HOW TO
LOVE
JESUS

Denny Thomas

ISBN 978-1-63630-851-7 (Paperback)
ISBN 978-1-63630-852-4 (Digital)

Copyright © 2021 Denny Thomas
All rights reserved
First Edition

All rights reserved. No part of this publication may be reproduced, distributed, or transmitted in any form or by any means, including photocopying, recording, or other electronic or mechanical methods without the prior written permission of the publisher. For permission requests, solicit the publisher via the address below.

Covenant Books, Inc.
11661 Hwy 707
Murrells Inlet, SC 29576
www.covenantbooks.com

CONTENTS

Preface 5

Why Was This Title Chosen? 7
Questions 13
How to Love Jesus Quiz 15
Questions and Answers with Comments 23
The Ten Commandments 57
How to Learn the Ten Commandments 59
The Ten Commandments with Comments 72
The Psalm of All Psalms 103
The Two Greatest Commandments 116
Pure Religion in the First Church 120
Pure Religion in the Church Today 122
What about the Money? 129

Final Word 131
Appendix A: How to Love Jesus Quiz Answers .. 134
Appendix B: Website References 138

PREFACE

Love is mentioned 310 times in the King James (Sword Study Bible). Love is the primary characteristic of God and is expressed plainly in John 3:16:

> "For God so loved the world, that He gave His only begotten Son, that whosoever believeth in Him should not perish, but have everlasting life."

As we accept Jesus, as our Lord and savior, we begin to fall in love with Him. We all have our own unique way to love Him. And, of course, we want our love to be received in a proper way and certainly with favor of the Lord. If we use the Bible as our only standard for how we practice our faith, also known as "Sola Scriptura," we cannot go wrong. Accordingly, the only data source for this writing is the King James Bible.

Sometimes, even when we give it our very best shot, we fail at loving others. Chances are, you have had the request to scratch the back of someone you loved dearly. As you scratched, the benefactor likely instructed you where to move across their back, ensuring maximum relief. It is the same way with the Lord, who tells us specifically *how* He wants us to love Him. I thought I loved the Lord, only to discover that I was way off the mark. Not until I discovered the words of the Lord Himself did I have an understanding of how to really love Him. I have found this one verse and from it came the title for this little book. I find it to be one of the most beautiful verses in all the scriptures. Yet, in all my years, I have never heard this verse preached or taught.

After discovering the verse on *how to love Jesus*, I continued searching for other verses that were associated with it. There were several verses showing the advantages of following, and others warning against the dangers of ignoring the verse. Presented in this writing are several of these verses, which also raise many questions.

As I write this in 2020, my internet searches for "How to Love Jesus" did not reveal this verse. It is as though it had been lost. But, such is not the case, and I am proud and honored to share it for the Lord in this writing. In doing so, many questions will arise and be answered. I will use italics, bold print, capital letters, and color to *shout* this wonderful secret of How to Love Jesus.

All profits from the sale of this book goes to widows and orphans.

WHY WAS THIS TITLE CHOSEN?

There are several verses in the Bible telling us to love God. How to actually do this is seldom preached or taught. Ask ten people to tell you how they love the Lord, and you will get ten different answers. Yet, the Bible only gives one answer to the question, and it seems like it has become a secret. This book is all about the secret of learning how to love Jesus. For me, it all started several years ago, with a small New Testament.

The answer to "How to Love Jesus" was discovered in the New Testament. It was not taken from a complete King James Bible because, in the beginning, all that was available to me was a small three-by-four-inch New Testament. From time to time, I would read various passages, noticing words like: "It is written…" (Matthew 4:4), and "If you love Me, keep My commandments" (John 14:15). I could not find where those words were written nor could I locate the commandments in the New Testament.

Shortly after being born, I was christened Catholic and grew up in a family that did not attend weekly church services. At best, we were C and E Christians, attending services only on Christmas and Easter. From time to time, I would ride with my neighbor who attended a Methodist church. At the age of fifteen, I was able to walk to a newly established local Baptist church, still carrying my little New Testament with me. A year and a half later, I answered an altar call, went forward, and professed my belief in Jesus Christ as my Lord and Savior. I was then baptized at the head of the Severn River in Maryland.

I carried that little New Testament with me when I joined the military in 1957. Years later, after finally getting a complete copy of the King James Bible, getting married, raising children, and completing several military assignments, I thought I should read the entire Bible. That idea kept getting kicked to the sidelines for many years due to the cares of life. After military retirement, divorce and without children to raise, and breaking all the commandments, it came to mind again that I have never read the complete Bible. I reasoned there was just so much to do and wondered who had the time to read it. Then it came to me. Wait a minute. I have time for *Field and Stream, Popular Mechanics, and Reader's Digest*, but I don't have time to read the Bible? It was time for a change.

My first change was to replace all of my reading material with a complete copy of the King James Bible. I would open the Bible, read a few verses, close the book, and leave. The next day, I would try to find out where I had left off to continue reading. Sometimes, I could not find where I had left off, so I started using a book marker. I continued reading, grasping only bits and pieces of information. I was not understanding very much. At this point, I decided I would read at least half a page per day instead of just a few verses. This went on for some time, and I realized I was getting a fuller picture. Soon after, I decided to read an entire chapter each day. I found that some days, the stories I read were so good that I continued to read over twelve chapters at a time. An example would be the story of Joseph. He was loved by his father yet hated by his brothers, who sold him into slavery. In spite of their actions, Joseph rose to power, second only to Pharaoh. What a beautiful story of love and mercy.

I struggled a great deal through the first reading, especially at trying to pronounce the many strange names. Not certain of how long it took me to read the Bible through the first time, I came to the end and thought, *What will I do now?* I decided to start over. This time, I was able to read chapter after chapter with greater ease. I finally found the words Jesus was referencing when He said, "It is written," and I discovered all the Ten Commandments, gaining a fuller understanding of the conceptual word of God. This daily reading was no longer just a task to get something accomplished. It became something I not only needed to do but looked forward to doing.

This went on for a few years. Each time I finished the book of Revelation and wondered what to do next, it was almost always the same—start again from the beginning. Except on one occasion, I decided to start over and look up every word I did not know. I would look it up in the dictionary. I do not recall how many words I looked up, but one stands out in remembrance. The word was *sabbath*. So I read the word *sabbath* in Exodus chapter 16 and thought about it. I finished my reading for the day, and that word lingered in my thoughts. I decided I did not need to look it up, as I already knew what it meant. It was Sunday. Nevertheless, I could not stop thinking about the word *sabbath*, and it was like a little voice telling me that I ought to look it up. So I got the *Webster's Dictionary* and looked up the word *sabbath*. It said: 1. The seventh day of the week, Saturday, as the day of rest and religious observance. I was stunned and very upset. I had been keeping Sunday as the sabbath all my life. How could this be? We went to Sunday school. We wore our Sunday best clothing. Was not the Lord raised on a Sunday? This could not be right. Something was really wrong here. I worried about this for a few days, even sharing my thoughts and concerns with my Baptist pastor who explained Sunday was the real sabbath. Then I went to the internet and discovered the true sabbath day. I learned that from the beginning, as the dictionary confirms, the sabbath day is really Saturday. Thank You, Father.

Besides the word *sabbath*, there were other words that I had misunderstood and looked up in the dictionary. The words were *fear, house, mark*, and *sign*.

I had a hard time understanding how I should fear the Lord and love Him at the same time. Most words have more than one meaning. To fear the Lord is to hold Him in high regard, high esteem, or awe. It does not mean to be afraid of Him.

Years ago, I lived in a house which would be described as a ranch-style house. In the gospel of John, I read where Jesus said, "In My Father's house are many mansions:...." (John 14:2) I could not understand how you could get or put many mansions into one house. Once again, my definition of the word *house* was different from that used in John's gospel. I found the correct meaning in the book of Exodus, where the Ten Commandments are given. In verse two, it says, "I am the Lord thy God, which have brought thee out of the land of Egypt, out of the house of bondage." Here, God is calling the land or country of Egypt a house. He is not describing the nation of Egypt as a single dwelling. Similarly, Jesus was not speaking of His Father's house as an individual dwelling. He uses the word *house* to refer to His Father's kingdom. The word *house* is used 2,026 times in the King James Bible.

The last two words that I misunderstood were *mark* and *sign*. It needs to be pointed out that they both mean the same thing. These words—fear, house, mark, and sign—are explained because they confused me for a long time. And since they are used repeatedly, I do not want to leave room for any confusion. They occur several times in this writing.

I would say I have read the Bible over twenty times from cover to cover. It is getting easier and faster to read since my children have put the King James Bible on my phone. I order a meal at a restaurant and read the Bible on my phone for ten minutes while I wait for my food to arrive. TV stations take breaks every fifteen minutes, and I can usually read a whole chapter during each break. Imagine how much reading could be accomplished during long waits at the doctor's office. I think anyone can read the King James Bible in a year if they want to.

One of the main reasons for the title of this book is because of the words found in Deuteronomy 6:4–5:

> "Hear, O Is'ra-el: The Lord our God *is* one Lord: and *thou shalt love the Lord* thy God with all thine heart, and with all thy soul, and with all thy might."
>
> (Emphasis mine)

Simply put, the Lord wants us to love Him. In fact, the Lord again mentions this in the New Testament with even stronger words. Mark 12:29 reads:

> "And Je'sus answered him, The first of all the commandments *is*, Hear, O Is'ra-el; The Lord our God is one Lord: and *thou shalt love the Lord* thy God with all thy heart, and with all thy soul, and with all thy mind, and with all thy strength: this *is* the first commandment."
> (Emphasis mine)

How can we read these words and not ask *how* can we best do this? *How to Love Jesus* will answer that very question. I have heard many people say they love the Lord, expressing they have a warm and wonderful feeling toward Him in their grateful heart. This is good, but is it good enough? Perhaps you may have said or thought you too loved the Lord. Are you sure? How do you know? Can you be certain? Be careful because the life of your soul depends on it.

QUESTIONS

Another purpose of *How to Love Jesus* is to answer all the following questions:

1. How do I know what the Lord, my God, wants me to do?
2. How do I go about doing what God wants me to do?
3. Can I get a sign from the Bible to make my faith stronger?
4. Can someone, ten feet away from me, tell if I am a Christian?
5. Where should God's Word be?
6. As a father or mother, what shall I do?

7–10. When should I say the Ten Commandments?

11. How else shall I promote the Ten Commandments?
12. Am I to write the Ten Commandments, and if so, where?
13. What is my righteousness?
14. What is the Word of God and where is it?
15. Where did Joshua put the book of the law?
16. Where did David say the Word of God was?
17. Where did Job get the commandments?
18. What should our delight be in?
19. How can I get wisdom?
20. Can I really be greatly delighted in the commandments?

21. What happens if someone despiseth the Word of God?
22. What happens when a person does not want to hear about the commandments?
23. What is the whole duty of man?
24. Won't my family and friends mock and ridicule me for following God's law?
25. What happens after you learn and teach the commandments to your children?
26. I have heard some of the commandments are outdated and do not apply today. Is that true?
27. What good thing shall I do that I may have eternal life?
28. Is there something I can do to love the Lord today?
29. Does the Lord know if I love Him or not?
30. Can God, the Father, love me, too?
31. Will Jesus ever love me?
32. Can God make Himself known to me?
33. How can I stay in love with Jesus?
34. How can I know the Lord?
35. I know John 3:16, "For God so loved the world, that He gave His only begotten Son…" What else does the Bible say He loves?
36. Can I be a member of the remnant church mentioned in the book of Revelation?
37. What is the testimony of Jesus Christ?
38. Is there a prophecy that still needs to be fulfilled?
39. Did Jesus ever mention any prophecy like this?
40. Can I eat of the tree of life?

HOW TO LOVE JESUS QUIZ

1. Are Christians required to keep the Lord's commandments?
   a. Yes
   b. No
   c. Yes, if they are aligned with the precepts of the church
   d. Yes, after the age of twelve, the age of understanding

2. The Lord's law, the Ten Commandments, shall be for a sign unto thee if they may be found in thy _____.
   a. Heart
   b. Bible
   c. Mouth
   d. Prayers

3. The Lord bids, commands, us to wear something on the border of our garments to help us remember the commandments. What is it?
   a. A tassel
   b. A fringe
   c. A double hem
   d. A ribbon of blue

4. Who should teach our children the Ten Commandments?
   a. Sunday School teachers
   b. Vacation Bible School volunteers
   c. Grandparents, for it is their primary purpose
   d. Their mothers and fathers

5. When should Christians speak about the commandments?
   a. When they lie down
   b. When they are sitting in their house
   c. When they are walking along the way
   d. When they rise up
   e. All of the above

6. Does the Bible tell us to write the commandments anywhere?
   a. Yes, we should write them on a card and carry them in our purses and wallets
   b. Yes, on the blank pages in the front and back of our bibles
   c. Yes, on the very front wall of each and every place of worship
   d. Yes, on the door post of our house

7. If we observe to do all God's commandments, it shall be our _____.
   a. Salvation
   b. Holiness
   c. Perfection
   d. Righteousness

8. How close is the word of God to us?
   a. In our mouths
   b. In our Bibles
   c. In our hearts
   d. Both a and c

9. Who was told that the book of the law should not depart from his mouth?
   a. Aaron
   b. Moses
   c. Job
   d. Joshua

10. Who said the word of God was in his tongue?
    a. David
    b. Ezra
    c. Melchizedek
    d. Mordecai

11. Who never turned back from the commandment of His lips?
    a. Job
    b. John the Baptist
    c. David
    d. Jacob

12. Blessed is the man that does which of these?
    a. Helps widows and orphans
    b. Keeps his word
    c. Delights in the law of the Lord
    d. Tithes one tenth of his income

13. The beginning of wisdom is which of these?
    a. The fear of the Lord
    b. Fulfilling the communion
    c. Being baptized
    d. Reading the entire Bible

14. What shall happen to those who despise the Word of God?
    a. They shall be destroyed
    b. They will spend eternity in purgatory
    c. They shall not lead the church to success
    d. They shall wander to and fro and be lost

15. What happens when a man turns his ear away from hearing the law?
    a. His wife shall be barren
    b. He will never learn the law
    c. He shall lead others astray
    d. His prayers shall be abomination

16. What is the whole duty of man?
    a. To do unto others as we allow them to do unto us
    b. To seek His face
    c. Fear God
    d. Keep His commandments
    e. Both c and d

---

17. Who said: "…My words which I have put in thy mouth shall not depart out of thy mouth,…?"
    a. Caiaphas the high priest
    b. Hezekiah
    c. Nebuchadnezzar
    d. The Lord

---

18. Jesus said He did not come to destroy the law or the prophets; instead, He came to:
    a. Fulfill them
    b. Explain their purposes
    c. Exemplify them
    d. Set the dates they were to start and stop

---

19. Whosoever shall do and teach the commandments shall be called what in the kingdom of heaven?
    a. Teacher
    b. Wise
    c. Great
    d. Savior

20. Jesus answered the young man, saying, "…but if thou will enter enter into life,… _____
    a. Follow Me
    b. Tithe twice as much if you are the first born receiving a double portion of the inheritance
    c. Join the priesthood
    d. Keep the commandments

21. "He that hath My commandments, and keepeth them… _____."
    a. He it is that loveth Me
    b. Shall be loved of My Father
    c. And I will love him
    d. And will manifest Myself to him
    e. All of the above

22. Jesus said you shall abide in His love if you do what?
    a. Pray often
    b. Keep His commandments
    c. Join a church and be baptized
    d. Ask forgiveness after each sin

23. The scripture says that we do know that we know Him if we?
    a. Continue to walk with Him
    b. Eat of His body and drink of His blood
    c. Pray thankfully all the time
    d. Keep His commandments

24. "For this is the love of God, _____."
    a. That none be lost
    b. That we all become disciples
    c. That we pray without ceasing
    d. That we keep His commandments

25. The book of Revelation says: "And the dragon was wroth with the woman, and went to make war with the remnant of her seed, which (fill in the blank), and have the testimony of Jesus Christ."
    a. Keep the commandments of God
    b. Keep Sunday holy
    c. Only eat clean meats
    d. Go to church on Holy day, Wednesday night Bible studies, and protect the women

26. The testimony of Jesus Christ is the spirit of _____?
    a. Love
    b. Prophecy
    c. Life and death
    d. Peace and prosperity

27. When the Lord returns, what happens just before we go to be with Him in heaven?
    a. We need to die first to find out
    b. The dead in Christ will rise first
    c. The dead know nothing
    d. The tares are separated from the wheat

28. Near the end of the book of Revelation, it says, "Blessed *are* they that do His commandments, that they may have right to _____."
    a. Keys to the pearly gates
    b. Everlasting life
    c. A new name and a white stone
    d. The tree of life

QUESTIONS AND ANSWERS WITH COMMENTS

The questions on page thirteen will be rewritten and then answered. The answers are taken from the scriptures in the King James Bible. After each answer, the author's comments are given.

1. How do I know what the Lord, my God, wants me to do?

> "Therefore shall ye keep My commandments, and do them: I *am* the LORD."
>
> (Leviticus 22:31)

Comment: Many people think the book of Leviticus is only for the priesthood. Such is not the case. There are many precepts in the book of Leviticus still as valid today as the day they were given. The precepts we no longer have to keep are the sacramental laws, which involved the cutting, bleeding, and killing of animals. The last bleeding for the remission of sins was done by our Lord and Savior, Jesus, on the cross.

2. How do I go about doing what God wants me to do?

> "For precept *must* be upon precept, precept upon precept; line upon line, line upon line; here a little, *and* there a little:"
> (Isaiah 28:10)

Comment: Most of the precepts in the King James Bible are in the Old Testament. The prophet Isaiah speaks of them and how we might find and use them. There is not a single list of precepts. They are found throughout the Bible. And we are to start doing them as we learn of them. There are precepts for many things, such as clean and unclean animals, sexual perversions, holiness, how to harvest a crop, gleaning, sowing a field with mixed seed, not to lie down with mankind or with any animal, fearing your parents, not being a talebearer, not eating blood, printing no marks upon yourself, and keeping the commandments. Precepts may also be found in the New Testament, addressing such topics as baptism and partaking of the Lord's Supper (communion).

3. Can I get a sign from the Bible to make my faith stronger?

> "And it shall be for a **sign** unto thee upon thine *hand*, and for a memorial between thine eyes, that the *LORD'S law* may be **in thy mouth**."
> (Exodus 13:9 Emphasis mine)

Comment: In the New Testament, the church leaders wanted Jesus to show them a sign. Remember, there was no New Testament at that time. All they had was the Old Testament. But did they read it? If they had, they would have found a sign. That sign is available to all of us today in Exodus 13:9.

Notice where this sign from the Lord is placed? upon the *hand*. Revelation 13: 16 says of Satan: "And he causeth all, both small and great, rich and poor, free and bond, to receive a mark in their right *hand*, or in their foreheads:" Again, notice where Satan wants to put his mark (sign). He wants to put it in the same place the Lord has already placed His sign of those that have His Ten Commandments *in their **mouth***.

Just as a man who is married to more than one woman at the same time still only wears one ring, this same concept applies here. If we learn the commandments and put them in our mouths and keep them, we will have the Lord's sign. You cannot have both of these signs on your hand at the same time. Choose the Lord's. Satan hates it and will flee away from us.

Notice that this verse is in Exodus chapter 13. Why is this interesting? Because the commandments are not given until seven chapters later in chapter 20. The commandments (law) have always been with us, long before Mount Sinai. Check out this verse, which occurred four hundred years before the Ten Commandments were given at Mount Sinai. It is in the story of Joseph, who was accused of adultery.

"But he refused, and said unto his master's wife, Behold, my master knew

> not what *is* with me in the house, and he hath committed all that he hath to my hand; *there is* none greater in this house than I; neither hath he kept back anything from me but thee, because thou *art* his wife: how then can I do this great wickedness, and **sin** against God?"
>
> (Genesis 39:8–9 Emphasis mine)

How did Joseph know adultery was a sin if the commandments were not given for another four hundred years? The Ten Commandments go further back in time, even to the very first family. God Himself speaks to Cain, saying:

> "If thou doest well, shalt thou not be accepted? And if thou doest not well, **sin** lieth at the door."
>
> (Genesis 4:7 Emphasis mine)

4. Can someone, ten feet away from me, tell if I am a Christian or not?

> "And the LORD spake unto Mo'ses, saying, Speak unto the children of Is'rael, and bid them that they make them fringes in the borders of their garments throughout their generations, and that they put upon the fringe of the borders **a ribbon of blue**: and it shall be unto you for a fringe, that ye may look upon it, **and remember** *all the commandments of the* LORD, and do them; and that ye seek not after your own heart

and your own eyes, after which ye use to go a whoring: **That ye may remember, and do all My commandments,** *and be holy unto your God."*

(Numbers 15:37 Emphasis mine)

Comment: Here is another precept that God directs His followers to do; however, it is rarely taught or performed in our churches today.

The word *bid* as used above means "to command." The purpose of the ribbon is that when you look upon it, you may remember God's Ten Commandments and do them.

A ribbon of blue attached to a man's suit jackets.

A ribbon of blue attached to a man's dress shirts.

A ribbon of blue attached to a man's Polo shirt.

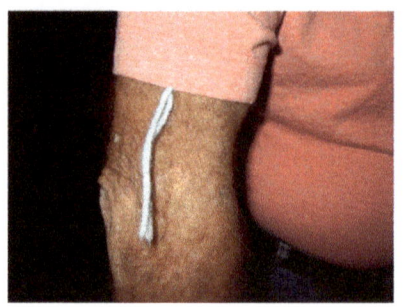

We are created in His image and are like Him in many ways. We need to be reminded of things from time to time. And so does God. Read the next verse carefully and see the similarity.

> "And it shall come to pass, when I bring a cloud over the earth, that the bow shall be seen in the cloud; And *I will* **remember** My covenant, which *is* between Me and you and every living creature of all flesh; and the waters shall no more become a flood to destroy all flesh. And the bow shall be in the cloud; and I will look upon it, *that I may* **remember** the everlasting covenant between God and every living creature of all flesh that *is* upon the earth."
> (Genesis 9:14 Emphasis mine)

5. Where should God's Word be?

> "And these words, which I command thee this day, shall be in thine heart:"
> (Deuteronomy 6:6)

Comment: God's words are to be respected and honored above all the words of man. They should be cherished, obeyed, and protected. Putting His word in your pocket or backpack is not as safe as putting them in the safe repository of your heart. For His glory and by His request, by precept, we put His words in our heart.

6. As a father or mother, what should I do?

> "And thou shalt teach them diligently unto thy children,…"
> (Deuteronomy 6:7)

Comment: If you took a survey, chances are you would not find more than one in ten persons who could recite the Ten Commandments word for word. This writer was not taught the commandments by his parents and did not learn them until the age of sixty-five. He did not ask his daughter to learn them until she was fifty-four years of age. We are never to old to do what God asks of us. It is the duty of the father and mother to teach each of their children the Ten Commandments.

7. When should I say the Ten Commandments?

> "…and shalt talk of them when thou sittest in thine house…"
> (Deuteronomy 6:7)

Comment: God enjoys hearing from all of us. Whether we are praying, giving thanks, or just reciting His commandments, He knows we are thinking of Him.

8. When should I say the Ten Commandments?

> "…and when thou walkest by the way…"
> (Deuteronomy 6:7)

Comment: We do not "walkest by the way" as much today as they did in days of old. But we sure do drive a lot. We often pray for safe passage but seldom bring the Lord's words with us on the trip. Reciting His commandments, while driving, is calming to oneself and pleasing to the Lord.

9. When should I say the Ten Commandments?

> "…and when thou liest down,…"
> (Deuteronomy 6:7)

Comment: Now I lay me down to sleep. I pray the Lord my soul to keep. Yes, we all need to remember our nightly prayers. But before you close your eyes, God wants to hear you say His beautiful commandments.

10. When should I say the Ten Commandments?

> "…and when thou riseth up…"
> (Deuteronomy 6:7)

Comment: When we open our eyes in the morning, God wants to hear from us again. Say His commandments for Him and step out of bed on the right footing.

11. How else shalt I promote the Ten Commandments?

> "And thou shalt bind them for a **sign** upon thine **hand**, and they shall be as frontlets between thine eyes."
> (Deuteronomy 6:8 Emphasis mine)

Comment: God wanted the Hebrew people to always keep His commandments in view and to continually preserve, protect, teach, and attend to them. The Hebrew nation was captured and taken to Babylon. After their return, they began to interpret this precept literally. They took this to mean to put various verses on parchment and place it in small leather boxes with straps. The boxes were to be worn on the forehead and left arm. Their misunderstanding and application was mentioned by Jesus in Matthew 23:5.

> "But all their works they do for to be seen of men: they make broad their phylacteries, and enlarge the boarders of their garments,…"

The primary purpose of these precepts was to cause the Hebrews to remember and keep all of God's commandments and to commemorate all of God's mighty works, which He did for them when He brought them out of Egypt. This purpose is expressed by the words preceding the commandments in Exodus 20:2.

> "I *am* the LORD thy God, which have brought thee out of the land of E'gypt, out of the house of bondage."

12. Am I to write the Ten Commandments and if so where?

> "And **thou shalt write them** upon the post of thy house…"
> (Deuteronomy 6:9 Emphasis mine)

Comment: The Bible tells of two occasions when God wanted His people to put something on the post of their house. The first time is found in Exodus 12: verse 22 and reads as follows:

> "And ye shall take a bunch of hyssop, and dip *it* in the blood that *is* in the basin, and strike the lintel and the two side post with the blood that *is* in the basin; and none of you shall go out at the door of his house until morning."

This is where God is telling them to take the blood of the Passover lamb and put it on the lintel and side post of their doors. When the Lord passed over and saw the blood on the doorpost, the destroyer was not sent in to kill the first-born child in that house. So here, for the second time, God is asking us to place something, His Ten Commandments, on the doorpost of our house.

But what about Christians and their thoughts on this precept today? Most Christians will tell you they are upset about what has been happening in the city square over the years regarding the Ten Commandments. They are not happy about the Ten Commandments being removed from one place after another all over our country. These are our fellow citizens who profess God, country, and family in this order. It is commendable that they place God first; however, they do not live by what they profess.

Here are three questions:

1) How many Christians in our country fly the American flag at their home?
2) How many of these same Christians have the Ten Commandments on their door post?
3) Are they really living with God first?

Even the pledge to our flag places God first with the words: "One nation under God."

13. What is my righteousness?

> "And it shall be our righteousness, if we observe to do all these commandments before the LORD our God, as He hath commanded us."
> (Deuteronomy 6:25)

Comment: Obeying God's Ten Commandments is the first step to righteousness.

14. What is the Word of God, and where is it?

> "But the word *is* very near unto thee, **in thy mouth**, and in thy heart, that thou mayest do it."
> (Deuteronomy 30:14 Emphasis mine)

Comment: There are 783,137 words in the King James Bible. God has asked us to memorize only the 296 words of His Ten Commandments.

Many people, even some Christians, think because this is an Old Testament precept, it does not apply today. However, Paul references this Old Testament verse in the New Testament:

> "But what saith it? The word is nigh thee, **even in thy mouth**, and in thy

heart: that is, the word of faith, which we preach;"
(Romans 10:8–9 Emphasis mine)

15. Where did Joshua put the book of the law?

> "This book of the law shall not depart out of thy **mouth**: but thou shalt meditate therein day and night,…"
> (Joshua 1:8 Emphasis mine)

Comment: Joshua will replace Moses and lead God's people into the promised land. And God speaks to Joshua in verse 8 and 9, saying:

> "This book of the law shall not depart out of thy **mouth**; but thou shall meditate therein day and night, that thou mayest observe to do according to all that is written therein: for then thou shalt make thy way prosperous, and then thou shalt have good success. Have not I commanded thee?"
> (Joshua 1:8–9 Emphasis mine)

16. Saying his last words, where did David say the Word of God was?

> "The Spirit of the LORD spake by me, and His word *was* **in my tongue**."
> (2 Samuel 23:2 Emphasis mine)

Comment: Samuel was a judge over Israel and also a prophet. He anointed David king and guided him in living for God. There should be no doubt that David knew the Ten Commandments and had them *in his mouth*.

17. Where did Job get the commandments?

> "Neither have I gone back from the commandment of His *lips*; I have esteemed the words of His *mouth* more than my necessary *food*."
> (Job 23:12 Emphasis mine)

Comment: God has spoken to many people like Adam, His prophets, all the people at the base of Mount Sinai, and could have certainly spoken them to Job. The book of Job is the oldest book in the King James Bible by some four hundred years, thus providing further evidence that the Ten Commandments have been here since our creation.

Did you notice the following?

Mouth in Exodus 13:9
Mouth in Deuteronomy 30:14
Mouth in Joshua 1:8
Tongue in 2 Samuel 23:2
Lips in Job 23:12

And again, in the New Testament, Paul writes in Romans 10:8, "But what saith it? The word is nigh thee, *even* in thy **mouth**, and in thy heart." *Six times* there is the connection or mention of the Ten commandments and having them *in our mouth*.

18. What should our delight be?

> "Blessed *is* the man that walketh not in the counsel of the ungodly, nor standeth in the way of sinners, nor sitteth in the seat of the scornful. But his delight *is* in the law of the LORD; and in His law doth he meditate day and night."
> (Psalm 1:1–2)

Comment: God's law was thought of as a real blessing. James, the brother of Jesus, wrote the following in James 1:25:

> "But whoso looketh into the perfect law of liberty, and continueth *therein*, he being not a forgetful hearer, but a doer of the work, this man shall be blessed in his deed."

And again in James 2:12, he writes:

> "So speak ye, and so do, as they that shall be judged by the law of liberty."

This is what we read earlier in Deuteronomy 6:7 regarding where and when we are to talk about the Ten Commandments, God's law. It explains what is meant by meditating in God's law day and night.

When we sittest in our house
When we walkest by the way
When we lie down
When we riseth up

19. How can I get wisdom?

> "The fear of the LORD *is* the beginning of wisdom: a good understanding have all they that do *His commandments*:"
> (Psalm 111.10)

Comment: Learning and living God's Ten Commandments is always the beginning. Consider when we sin and learn of it, we become regretful and afflicted. We ask God's forgiveness and start over by going back to keeping His commandments.

20. Can I really be greatly delighted in God's Ten Commandments?

> "Praise ye the LORD. Blessed *is* the man *that* feareth the LORD, *that* delighteth greatly in His commandments."
> (Psalm 112:1)

Comment: Imagine what our world would be like if:

No one stole anything
No one committed adultery
No on used the Lord's name in vain
No one killed another person
(including abortions)

No one lied
No one coveted another's belongings
No one worshiped man-made idols (statues)
Everyone honored their father and mother
Everyone rested from their work on the sabbath day
Everyone worshiped the Lord Jesus only

Think of it. No need for locks and keys. Police only direct traffic. Thousands of families remain together. The Lord's name is held in honor around the world. Thousand upon thousands of people are still alive from not being murdered. Millions of hearts avoid being broken from lies. No wars because nations did not covet other nations' land. No security systems for our homes, cars, and computers. No one would be in credit card debt because of coveting. The entire world would give praise, honor, thanks, and glory to God on the sabbath day all at the same time. Wombs would be fruitful as a result of the abolishment of abortion. Yes, the world would surely be a much better place. How could we not delight greatly in a world such as this compared to what we live in today?

21. What happens if someone despiseth the Word of God?

"Whoso despiseth the word shall be destroyed: but he that feareth the commandment shall be rewarded."
(Proverbs 13:13)

Comment: There are only two types of relationships a person can have with God. It is either love or hate. Part of the second commandment mentions this:

> "...for I the LORD thy God *am* a jealous God, visiting the iniquity of the fathers upon the children unto the third and fourth *generation* of them that hate Me; And showing mercy unto thousands of them that love Me and keep My commandments."
>
> (Exodus 20:5–6)

22. What happens when a person does not want to hear about the commandments?

> "He that turneth away his ear from hearing the law, even his prayer *shall be* abomination."
>
> (Proverbs 28:9)

Comment: Turning away the ear in more than not having the time to listen to someone speak about the commandments. It is also when we know about a commandment and continue to do otherwise. It is a rejection of God's Word itself. An example would be the fourth commandment. Most churches do not keep the seventh day Sabbath. Some say it does not make a difference which day we keep as our Sabbath. They call some other day the

Lord's Day. But they fail to understand the words of the fourth commandments itself. Exodus 20:10 reads:

> …But the seventh day *is* the sabbath of the LORD thy God:…

Only the *seventh day* is His Sabbath. Only that day did He hallow and bless. Any other day claimed by man to be the Sabbath is surely not blessed as such by our God.

The Bible says we have all sinned. Some know they sin and very much enjoy its pleasures with no intent to stop. Using drugs is an example. Many people wait until they are at the end of their rope before calling on the Lord for help. This verse is a promise or prophecy to all those who deliberately turn from His commandments. His ear is not turned toward them.

23. What is the whole duty of man?

> "Let us hear the conclusion of the whole matter: Fear God, and keep His commandments: for this *is* the whole *duty* of man."
>
> (Ecclesiastes 12:13)

Comment: Ecclesiastes was written by King Solomon during the time of his reign, long before the arrival of Jesus in the New Testament. Jesus teaches us to include baptism, the Lord's Supper (communion), and a new commandment to love one another.

24. Won't my family and friends mock and ridicule me for following God's law?

> "Hearken unto Me, ye that know righteousness, the people in whose heart *is* My law, fear ye not the reproach of men, neither be ye afraid of their reviling."
>
> (Isaiah 51:7)

Comment: When we worry about other people's opinion of us, we are being prideful. Overcoming our pride is a giant step in maturing as a Christian. Do not let your pride prevent you from obeying His commandments or precepts. Let pride for the Lord overcome the fear of what others think. He will bear your reproach, and you need not be afraid. He will bear any feelings you may have like embarrassment or shame.

25. What happens after you learn and teach the Ten Commandments to your children?

> "As for Me, this *is* My covenant with them, **saith the LORD**; My spirit that *is* upon thee, and **My words which I have put in thy mouth,** shall not depart out of thy *mouth*, nor out of the *mouth* of thy seed, nor out of the *mouth* of thy seed's seed, **saith the LORD**, from henceforth and forever."
>
> (Isaiah 59:21 Emphasis mine)

> Mouth, Exodus 13:9
> Mouth, Deuteronomy 30:14
> Mouth, Joshua 1:8
> Tongue, 2 Samuel 23:2
> Lips, Job 23:12
> Mouth, Romans 10:8
> Mouth, Isaiah 59:21

Note: This is the **seventh** time we are reminded of the Lord's law being in **our mouth**.

Comment: Another name for Jesus is Emmanuel, which means "God with us." That name was given before Jesus was born. And so He lived, was crucified, buried, rose again on the third day, and stayed with man forty days before ascending up to heaven. Knowing He would not remain here with man, He promised this in John 14:26:

> "But the Comforter, *which is* the Ho'ly Ghost, whom the Father will send in My name, He shall teach you all things, and bring all things to your remembrance, whatsoever I have said unto you."

It is His Holy Spirit encouraging you to inquire and study, and He will support you in learning all things. Remember in Deuteronomy 6:6, it said you are to teach the Ten Commandments to your children? As parents, this is what we should do. You learn the Ten Commandments. You teach them to your children, and they do likewise and teach the Ten Commandments to their children. Hence, the words that he has put in our mouths shall not depart out of our mouths for many generations.

Read Isaiah 59:21 again and notice carefully what the Lord is saying about where He is placing His words. Once again, for the seventh time from the scriptures: **"in thy mouth."**

But be cautious. As much as God wants you to learn His commandments, the evil one, Satan, will hinder your every efforts to learn them. It is he that tells you the process is too difficult. It is he that tells you not to worry because most people don't know them anyway.

Before we look at the next question, answer, and comment, we need to see three other verses to prepare ourselves to better understand the complete answer to the question.

> "For behold, I create new heavens and a new earth: and the former shall not be remembered, nor come to mind."
> (Isaiah 65:17)

> "For as the new heaven and the new earth, which I will make, shall remain before Me, saith the LORD, so shall your seed and your name remain."
> (Isaiah 66:22)

> "And I saw a new heaven and a new earth: for the first heaven and the first

earth were passed away; and there was no more sea."

(Revelation 21:1)

26. I have heard some of the Ten Commandments are outdated and do not apply today. Is that true?

> "Think not that I am come destroy the law, or the prophets: I am not come to destroy, but to fulfill. For verily I say unto you, Till heaven and earth pass, one jot or one tittle shall in no wise pass from the law, till all be fulfilled. Whosoever therefore shall break one of these least commandments, and shall teach men so, he shall be called the least in the kingdom of heaven: but whosoever shall do and teach *them*, the same shall be called great in the kingdom of heaven."
>
> (Matthew 5:17–19)

Comment: The Lord Jesus validates all of His commandments, reassuring us that they are as applicable today as the day they were given at Mount Sinai. The Ten Commandments are His, and He has never changed them. No pastor, pope, potentate, preacher, or president has ever been authorized by God to alter, change, or amend any of His commandments. Every man or woman who decides to minister for Christ better fully understand their responsibilities for doing and teaching all of God's commandments and precepts as they are written in the King James Bible.

Perhaps you have seen where the Ten Commandments have been abbreviated and sold on placards and posters. In many cases, the fourth commandments is expressed simply as:

"Remember the sabbath day, to keep it holy."
(Exodus 20:8)

However, the fourth commandment continues on through verse 11. The Lord explains how to keep the Sabbath day holy.

He instructs us in verses 9 through 11:

"Six days shalt thou labor, and do all thy work: But the seventh day *is* the sabbath of the LORD thy God: *in it* thou shalt not do any work, thou, nor thy son, nor thy daughter, thy manservant, nor thy maidservant, nor thy cattle, nor thy stranger that *is* within thy gates: For *in* six days the LORD made heaven and earth, the sea, and all that in them *is*, and rested the seventh day: wherefore the LORD blessed the sabbath day, and hallowed it."

A part of something is only a part. We are not commanded to keep only a part of any commandment. This is like telling a half-truth, and there is no half-truth with God. God is very clear on this in the following verses.

"Ye shall not add unto the word which I command you, neither shall ye

diminish *ought* from it, that ye may keep the commandments of the LORD your God which I command you."
(Deuteronomy 4:2)

"What thing soever I command you, observe to do it: thou shalt not add thereto, nor diminish from it."
(Deuteronomy 12:32)

27. What good thing shall I do, that I may have eternal life?

"…but if thou wilt enter into life, keep the commandments."
(Matthew 19:17)

Comment: To break or not keep any one of the Ten Commandments is a sin and the wages of sin is death. By knowing and doing the Ten Commandments, we can be sinless and worthy of eternal life after the resurrection.

28. Is there something I can do to love Him today?

"If you love Me, keep My commandments."
(John 14:15)

Comment: Although this is written in the New Testament, it is not new. In the second commandment (Old Testament), it says:

"And showing mercy unto thousands of them that love Me, and keep My commandments."
(Exodus 20:6)

There are no secrets with Jesus. He has shared with us all we need to know.

29. Does the Lord know if I love Him or not?

> He that hath My commandments, and keepeth them, he it is that loveth Me:...
>
> (John 14:21)

Comment: Notice there are two parts to this. First, in order to love the Lord, a person must "hath" the commandments. That means to have them within ourselves. Having them written in a book that collects dust on the coffee table does not get the job done. We are not just required to read the commandments, we are to know each word by heart. Knowing them by heart shows the person you are teaching them to that they may also master learning the Ten Commandments. You are proof that remembering the commandments can be accomplished. Second, we must keep them. This is the *how* to love Jesus. This is how Jesus wants us to love Him.

30. Can God the Father love me also?

> "He that hath My commandments, and keepeth them, he it is that loveth Me: and he that loveth Me **shall be loved of My Father,...**"
>
> (John 14:21 Emphasis mine)

Comment: Think about this for a moment. Did God the Father love His Son, Jesus? John 14:21 says that you will be loved of His Father, which is the same love that He has for His only Son.

31. Will Jesus ever love me?

> He that hath My commandments, and keepeth them, he it is that loveth Me: and he that loveth Me shall be loved of My Father, **and I will love him**,…"
> (John 14:21 Emphasis mine)

Comment: Everyone wants to be loved. Everyone wants to hear those three precious words: "I love you." Well, here it is from God the Father and His son, Jesus.

32. Can God make Himself known to me?

> "He that hath My commandments, and keepeth them, he it is that loveth Me: and he that loveth Me shall be loved of My Father, and I will love him, **and will manifest myself to him.**"
> (John 14:21 Emphasis mine)

Comment: Jesus will manifest Himself to us if we have and keep His commandments. His word will be made clearer to us, and we will learn and grow much faster spiritually. Knowing the Ten Commandments is knowing Christ Jesus. Keeping them is keeping Him. As we read through our Bible, we come to Deuteronomy 6:4–5, which gives us a very important precept. Again, it reads:

> "Hear, O Is'ra-el: The LORD our God *is* one LORD: And **thou shalt love the LORD thy God** with all thine heart, and with all thine soul, and with all thine might."
>
> (Emphasis mine)

How to rightfully fulfill the need of loving God, in Deuteronomy 6:4–5, is perfectly answered in **John 14:21**.

This is the ideal way to love Jesus.

John 14:21 is How to Love Jesus.

I am an old man now and can honestly say I have never heard this verse, John 14:21, mentioned, preached, or taught during a church service or on TV. This being the case, I am both delighted and honored to share it in this writing. Thank You, Jesus. John 14:21 shall be rewritten here, in bold, large capital letters, that it might be shouted to the world.

> "HE THAT HATH MY COMMANDMENTS AND KEEPETH THEM, HE IT IS THAT LOVETH ME: AND HE THAT LOVETH ME SHALL BE LOVED OF MY FATHER, AND I WILL LOVE HIM AND MANIFEST MYSELF TO HIM."
> **(John 14:21 Emphasis mine)**

33. How can I stay in love with Jesus?

> "If ye keep My commandments, ye shall abide in My love; even as I have kept My Father's commandments, and abide in His love."
>
> (John 15:10)

Comment: Notice the word *shall* in this verse. If Jesus said you shall, then you certainly shall abide in His love. Keeping His commandments gets easier every day.

34. How can I know the Lord?

> "And hereby we do know that we know Him, if we keep His commandments."
>
> (1 John 2:3)

Comment: His commandments are more than His word in us. They are also His will for us. As Christ lives, so do His commandments. The Ten Commandments are not dead but alive. Living every day, in us, through our worship and obedience. The commandments are learned, lived, memorized, practiced, spoken of, studied, taught, and written every day.

35. I know John 3:16, "For God so loved the world, that He gave His only begotten Son..." What else does the Bible say He loves?

> "For this is the love of God, that we keep His commandments: and His commandments are not grievous."
>
> (1 John 5:3)

Comment: Do you ever go to bed on a cold winter's night and slip between the cool sheets on the bed, warming them with your body, when it strikes you? You forgot to put the cat out or place the trash can on the curb. That is grievous. But no one goes to bed and bolts upright thinking: *Dog gone it! I forgot to kill someone today.* Nor does anyone wake up thinking: *Man, what a great day, I just can't wait to stick up a seven eleven.* To the contrary, as these acts are naturally repulsive to us and are grievous thoughts. Therefore, the commandments are not grievous to us. The commandments are themselves a blessing to us.

36. Can I be a member of the remnant church mentioned in the book of Revelation?

> "And the dragon was wroth with the woman, and went to make war with the remnant of her seed, which keep the commandments of God, and have the testimony of Je'sus Christ."
>
> (Revelation 12:17)

Comment: The book of Revelation has a lot of imagery and scares many readers. Here, we will break down this verse.

The dragon is the devil or Satan.
Was *wroth* means he was very angry with the woman.
The woman is the church.
Satan goes to make war with the remnant of her seed.
Her seed represents the members of the church.
The remnant members are those who:
Keep the commandments of God and
Have the testimony of Jesus Christ.

Let's say there are a hundred members in the church. Less than half know and keep God's Ten Commandments (the remnant). Notice Satan only wants to make war against the members of the church that keep God's commandments. This is because keeping the commandments is, in itself, worshiping and honoring our God. Satan wants that worship to stop. He wants that worship toward himself. Notice also Satan does not go after the majority of the members. He already has them on his side because they do not know and keep the Ten Commandments of our God.

37. What is the testimony of Jesus Christ?

> "...for the testimony of Je'sus is the spirit of prophecy."
> (Revelation 19:10)

Comment: Prophecy is the prediction of events to come. Our faith is strengthened when we read of a prophecy that has been or is being fulfilled or completed. The many fulfilled prophecies in the Old and New Testaments reinforce our trust and faith in the prophets and the Lord Jesus.

38. Is there a prophecy that still needs to be fulfilled?

> "For the Lord Himself shall descend from heaven with a shout, with the voice of the archangel, and with the trump of God: and the dead in Christ shall rise first: Then we which are alive *and* remain shall be caught up together with them in the clouds, to meet the Lord in the air: and so shall we ever be with the Lord. Wherefore comfort one another with these words."
> (1 Thessalonians 4:16–18)

Comment: This prophecy is our hope and promise for Christ's return. He is coming to receive us along with those that believed in Him and have passed on before us.

39. Did Jesus ever mention any prophecy like this?

> "In My Father's house are many mansions: if *it were* not *so*, I would have told you. I go to prepare a place for you. And if I go and prepare a place for you, I will come again, and receive you unto Myself; that where I am, *there* ye may be also."
>
> (John 14:2–3)

Comment: Here, the Lord Jesus lets us know we will certainly meet each other, just like the previous verse in question thirty-eight. We also learn that the Lord is preparing a place for us.

Let's look back at the answer to question thirty-two. John 14:21 mentions that the Lord will manifest Himself to us if we have His commandments and keep them. Look again at John 14:2–3 and notice the highlighted words.

> "In My Father's house are many mansions: if *it were* not *so*, **I** would have told **you**. **I** go to prepare a place for **you**. And if **I** go and prepare a place for **you**, **I** will come again, and receive **you** unto Myself; that where **I** am, there **ye** may be also."
>
> (John 14:2–3 Emphasis mine)

The Bible is a love letter from God to you and me.

This is a very personal *prophecy* from God directly to *you*. Notice who is in this verse of prophecy. Just *you* and Jesus. He mentions *you* five times. He mentions *Himself* the same number of times. There is no one else mentioned, just *you* and Jesus.

That is the way our relationship should be with the lord. It must be a one-on-one relationship. Think about it. Who can repent for you? Who can be baptized for you? Who can partake of the Lord's Supper for you? No one. Each of us needs to have that personal, one-on-one relationship with Jesus.

40. Can I eat of the tree of life?

> "Blessed *are* they that do His commandments, that they may have right to the tree of life, and may enter in through the gates into the city."
> (Revelation 22:14)

Comment: The Bible begins with the creation of all things by God, including a garden with the tree of life. The Bible ends mentioning again the availability of the tree of life. Notice also that the commandments have always been with us, are with us today, and will be with us as we "enter in through the gates into the city."

THE TEN COMMANDMENTS

I. Thou shalt have no other gods before Me.
II. Thou shalt not make unto thee any graven image, or any likeness *of any thing* that *is* in heaven above, or that *is* in the earth beneath, or that *is* in the water under the earth: Thou shalt not bow down thyself to them, nor serve them: for I the LORD thy God *am* a jealous God, visiting the iniquity of the fathers upon the children unto the third and fourth *generation* of them that hate Me; And showing mercy unto thousands of them that love Me, and keep My commandments.
III. Thou shalt not take the name of the LORD thy God in vain; for the LORD will not hold him guiltless that taketh His name in vain.
IV. Remember the sabbath day, to keep it holy. Six days shalt thou labor, and do all thy work: But the seventh day *is* the sabbath of the LORD thy God: *in it* thou shalt not do any work, thou, nor thy son, nor thy daughter, thy manservant, nor thy maidservant, nor thy cattle, nor thy stranger that *is* within thy gates: For in six days the LORD made heaven and earth, the sea, and all that in them *is*, and rested the seventh day: wherefore the LORD blessed the sabbath day, and hallowed it.
V. Honor thy father and thy mother: that thy days may be long upon the land which the LORD thy God giveth thee.
VI. Thou shalt not kill.

VII. Thou shalt not commit adultery.
VIII. Thou shalt not steal.
IX. Thou shalt not bear false witness against thy neighbor.
X. Thou shalt not covet thy neighbor's house, thou shalt not covet thy neighbor's wife, nor his manservant, nor his maidservant, nor his ox, nor his ass, nor anything that *is* thy neighbor's.

HOW TO LEARN THE TEN COMMANDMENTS

"Thy hands have made me and fashioned me: give me understanding, that I may learn Thy commandments."
(Psalm 119:73)

There is an old twelfth century proverb by John Heywood. I am sure you have heard it before. It goes like this: "You can lead a horse to water, but you can't make him drink." It means you can do a lot to help people do something, but you cannot make them do it.

Another primary purpose of this little book is to encourage and equip the reader to learn the Ten Commandments, because that is a prerequisite for really loving God. Remember John 14:21. "He that hath my commandments, and keepeth them, he it is that loveth Me." By learning the commandments and keeping them, you may truthfully answer *yes* to the question the Lord asked Peter three times in John 21:15–17, "…lovest thou Me…?"

So, I lead the horse to water, but I can't make him drink. Truthfully, making him drink is not my job. My real job is to lead him to the water and *make him thirsty*. Making him drink is the job of the Holy Spirit. And so it is with anyone learning the Ten Commandments.

Look at what has happened so far. You saw a little book. You saw the title. It touched your mind and heart. It caused you to examine yourself and your love for the Lord. You meditated, pondered, and wondered about it. You had to know the truth to this question, so you bought the little book. It is the Holy Spirit drawing you, convincing you to learn how God wants you to love Him by learning and keeping His Ten Commandments.

Learning the Ten Commandments is more than a ten-minute job. It may take weeks to learn them. It took the author seven days to learn them using several of the methods described below.

1. Have a copy of the Ten Commandments available for review. Better yet, keep a copy of the verse (or portion of verse) you are practicing handy.
2. Allow time for this study. Avoid multitasking, as it does not aid in remembering anything. It is best to focus on one thing at a time. Turn off the TV and cell phone. Yes, they still have *off* buttons.
3. As it took you more than one sitting to learn your *ABCs* and your multiplication tables, so it will be with memorizing the Ten Commandments. Do not try to memorize all the commandments at once. You will have little success this way and make yourself more frustrated than ever. It is like eating a pie. Eat a slice, or maybe even two. You're okay. But if you eat the entire pie, problems may arise. You may feel too full and need to lie down. You may not feel well. Why? Because you ate it all at once. Learn the commandments in bite-size pieces.

4. Do not mix the commandments or jump from one to another.
5. Learn them in their proper sequence.
6. As you commit each commandment to memory, continue repeating them often. If they are not repeated often, you will forget them quickly.
7. As you are memorizing the commandments, meditate on what the words are telling you. Try to understand what you learn. Things that you understand are memorized nine times faster. Keep doing this until you have memorized all Ten Commandments.
8. Test yourself from time to time. One way to test yourself is to write down the commandments and compare your writing with Exodus chapter 20. Once again, writing them down reinforces memorization and learning.
9. Record your voice reciting the commandments and verify them with Exodus chapter 20. If your recitation is correct, you can listen to your recording while doing the laundry or driving your car.
10. Teach the commandments to another person.
11. When frustration enters the scene, take a break. Get away from it for a while.
12. Remind yourself that you are not failing; you are learning.
13. If frustration persist with a particular portion, shorten the chunk you are working on.
14. Have a friend join you in learning the commandments. You could recruit a distant friend and repeat verses back and forth to one another over the phone. A person having the same goal in mind can give you support.

Learning and committing the Ten Commandments to total recall is a hard job. And you want to learn them for many reasons. You want to succeed and be perfect. As you study, apply all your abilities and all of what you already know, remembering:

1. Prayer and Practice.
   "And all things, whatsoever ye shall ask in prayer, believing, ye shall receive."

   (Matthew 21:22)

2. You are not alone.
   "But the Comforter, *which is* the Ho'ly Ghost, whom the Father will send in My name, He shall teach you all things, and bring all things to your remembrance, whatsoever I have said unto you."

   (John 14:26)

3. You can do it.
   "I can do all things through Christ which strengtheneth me."

   (Philippians 4:13)

Learning the First Commandment

Exodus 20:3 holds the first commandment.

I **"Thou shalt have no other gods before Me."**

This is a very simple and straightforward command. Let this be your day's work for the first day. Repeat it to yourself over and over. Bless your supper and repeat the first commandment. As you watch TV, repeat the first commandment at the beginning of each commercial break. When you go to the mailbox, repeat the first commandment. Go to the bathroom, repeat the first commandment. Step into the shower, repeat the first commandment. After your nightly prayers, repeat the first commandment. When you wake up, stay still and repeat the first commandment.

So what did you accomplish on the first day? You learned the first commandment? No, no, no. You accomplished much more! You just started fulfilling Deuteronomy 6:7, which, in part says, "…And shalt talk of them when thou sittest in thine house, and when thou walkest by the way, and when thou liest down, and when thou risest up." Although the commandments were written in stone, they are very much alive today. We write them, we say them, we teach them, we practice them, we do them, and we love them.

Learning the Second Commandment

So you have the first commandment down pat, and now you're ready to start on the second commandment, which is:

II **"Thou shalt not make unto thee any graven image, or any likeness *of any thing* that *is* in heaven above, or that *is* in the earth beneath, or that *is* in the water under the earth: Thou shalt not bow down thyself to them, nor serve them: For I the LORD thy God *am* a jealous God, visiting the iniquity of the fathers upon the children unto the third and fourth *generation* of them that hate Me; And showing mercy unto thousands of them that love Me and keep My commandments."**

(Exodus 20:4–6)

Wow! This is a very long commandment. This is where most people give up in frustration. It is just too much pie. Here is a solution: *chunking*. This method allows you to divide the commandment into smaller chunks. So, look at the second commandment and take a small slice. Let's take this much:

> "Thou shalt not make unto thee any graven image, or any likeness *of any thing*"

Before you start practicing the second commandment, always recite the first commandment. This is the same pattern as outlined in Isaiah 28:10, "For precept *must be* upon precept, precept upon precept; line upon line, line upon line; here a little, *and* there a little:"

To begin the second commandment, we would say:

> "Thou shalt have no other gods before Me. Thou shalt not make unto thee any graven image, or any likeness *of any thing*."

This is enough for right now. It is just a matter of reciting it over and over until you are satisfied you have it down pat. Once you are happy with your progress, go ahead and take another chunk or slice of the pie. If it takes three or four days, it is okay. Again, think back on how long it took you to remember your *ABC*'s.

The next chunk might be:

"that *is* in the heaven above, or that *is* in the earth beneath, or that *is* in the water under the earth."

Continue using the following chunks to complete the second commandment.

"Thou shalt not bow down thyself to them, nor serve them:

for I the LORD thy God *am* a jealous God,

visiting the iniquity of the fathers upon the children

unto the third and fourth *generation* of them that hate Me;

And showing mercy unto thousands of them that

love Me, and keep My commandments."

Congratulations! You did it. Good job. You just conquered the greatest stumbling block to memorizing all ten of the commandments. It alone contains over 30 percent of all the words in the commandments. This is where most people give up with thoughts like: *I can't do it. It's too long. It's too hard. I am too old. It's okay if I fail.* It sounds like someone is pulling you away from learning the commandments. This is sinking thinking by none other than Satan himself.

FAIL = First Attempt in Learning

Learning the Third Commandment

The third commandment is:

III **"Thou shalt not take the name of the LORD thy God in vain; for the LORD will not hold him guiltless that taketh His name in vain."**
(Exodus 20:7)

Remember to recite the first and second commandment before beginning the third. The first chunk for the third commandment could be:

"Thou shalt not take the name of the LORD thy God in vain;"

Followed by the second chunk.

"for the LORD will not hold him guiltless that taketh His name in vain."

Great job! You are almost a third of the way to completing the goal of learning the Ten Commandments.

Learning the Fourth Commandment

By now, the first and second commandments are securely fastened in your memory because you have reinforced them over and over. Both processes of repeating and chunking are working. When learning any new commandment, always start with the first and reciting your way up to your new chunk line. Here is the fourth commandment.

> **IV** "Remember the sabbath day, to keep it holy. Six days shalt thou labour, and do all thy work: But the seventh day *is* the sabbath of the LORD thy God: *in it* thou shalt not do any work, thou, nor thy son, nor thy daughter, thy manservant, nor thy maidservant, nor thy cattle, nor thy stranger that *is* within thy gates: For *in* six days the LORD made heaven and earth, the sea, and all that in them *is*, and rested the seventh day: wherefore the LORD blessed the sabbath day, and hallowed it."
>
> (Exodus 20:8–11)

Despite containing more words than any of the other commandments, the fourth is very easy to learn for two reasons: it tells a story, and the chunking is easy to do. The chunks are:

"Remember the sabbath day, to keep it holy.

Six days shalt thou labour,
and do all thy work:

But the seventh day *is* the sabbath
of the LORD thy God:

in it thou shalt not do any work,

thou, nor thy son, nor thy daughter,

thy manservant, nor thy maidservant,

> nor thy cattle, nor thy stranger
> that *is* within thy gates:
>
> For *in* six days the LORD
> made heaven and earth,
>
> the sea, and all that in them *is*,
>
> and rested the seventh day:
>
> wherefore the LORD blessed the
> sabbath day, and hallowed it."

There are 296 words in the Ten Commandments. If you have memorized the first four commandments, you have memorized 221 of them. Put another way, you have completed 75 percent of your goal. Good job.

Learning the Fifth Commandment

The next four commandments are pretty easy and do not require much chunking. Recite the first four commandments and begin the fifth, which is:

> **V** **"Honor thy father and thy mother: that thy days may be long upon the land which the LORD thy God giveth thee."**

(Exodus 20:12)

Use as the first chunk:

> "Honor thy father and thy mother

Followed by the second:

> that thy days may be long upon the land which the LORD thy God giveth thee."

Learning the Sixth Commandment

The sixth commandment is the first of the shortest commandments. Simply repeat the first five commandments and this single chunk.

VI "Thou shalt not kill."

(Exodus 20:13)

Learning the Seventh Commandment

After saying the first six commandments, add this one chunk to it, and soon you will be working on number eight.

VII "Thou shalt not commit adultery."

(Exodus 20:14)

Learning the Eighth Commandment

The eighth commandment is also a single chunk. Include it after repeating the first seven commandments.

VIII "Thou shalt not steal."

(Exodus 20:15)

Learning the Ninth Commandment

Like the eighth commandment, the ninth has only one chunk, which is:

IX "Thou shalt not bear false witness against thy neighbor."

(Exodus 20:16)

Learning the Tenth Commandment

The tenth commandment has thirty-three words and needs to be broken into chunks. The tenth commandment is:

X "Thou shalt not covet thy neighbor's house, thou shalt not covet thy neighbor's wife, nor his manservant, nor his maidservant, nor his ox, nor his ass, nor anything that *is* thy neighbor's."

(Exodus 20:17)

After saying the first nine commandments, add the needed chunks in this order:

Thou shalt not covet thy neighbor's house,

thou shalt not covet thy neighbor's wife,

nor his manservant, nor his maidservant,

nor his ox, nor his ass,

nor anything that *is* thy neighbor's.

Here is another way for the minister, pastor, or preacher to teach the Ten Commandments to their church members. As you open every service, go to the podium with your King James Bible opened to Exodus chapter 20. Ask the assembly to arise with their King James Bibles opened to the same passage. And together, slowly and aloud, read verses 3 through 17. Do not, I repeat, do not stand in front of the congregation *without* your open Bible before you. Otherwise, you may be perceived as a showoff or better-than-thou. Before long, you will notice members of the flock arising and repeating the commandments without using their Bibles. Hallelujah!

It seems every sermon includes time to gather tithes. Which do you think God really prefers? The tithes? Or would He prefer His flock to learn His Ten Commandments, especially since it only takes two minutes to say them. Before you answer, read Matthew 5:19, paying close attention to the last two lines.

"Whoso therefore shall break one of these least commandments, and shall teach men so, he shall be called the least in the kingdom of heaven: but whosoever shall do and *teach them, the same shall be called great* in the kingdom of heaven."

(Emphasis mine)

We don't learn the commandments to be saved.
We learn them because we are saved.

THE TEN COMMANDMENTS WITH COMMENTS

At the end of the book of Genesis, God sent a savior to rescue the Hebrew and Egyptian nations from a great seven-year famine. His name was Joseph; he interpreted King Pharaoh's dream and became second only to the king in all of Egypt. In time, the people of this generation passed away, and new men ruled Egypt. They feared the Hebrew nation might become greater and overthrow them. So they put them under bondage, forcing them to build cities for the new Pharaoh.

For four hundred years, the Hebrew people were held in bondage by Pharaoh, king of Egypt. During that entire time, they were also influenced by Egyptian religious practices and their many gods, such as Ra, the supreme solar god; Isis, the goddess of love; Tefnut, the goddess of rain; Nut, the goddess of the sky; Shu, the god of the wind; Geb, the god of earth and vegetation; and Osiris, the god of death.

God saw all that was happening and wanted to free His chosen people from the oppression of hard labor and the abomination of the Egyptian gods and religious practices. So, God sent another savior, whose name was Moses. Through Moses, God saved the Hebrews by performing many signs and wonders against Egypt. God sent plaque upon plaque of blood, frog, lice, flies, dead animals, boils, hail, locusts, darkness, and ultimately, the death of the firstborn of every Egyptian family and even their cattle. God also performed miracle after miracle, including sparing the Israelites from the plaque of death (known as the Passover) and the parting of the Red Sea, which swallowed up Israel's enemies.

In order to help Moses rebuild the Hebrew nation, God gave His people the Ten Commandments to show them His way, that they might live and not sin against the Lord or one another.

The First Commandment

I   **"Thou shalt have no other gods before Me."**
(Exodus 20:3)

"Ye shall not make with Me gods of silver, neither shall ye make unto you gods of gold."
(Exodus 20:23)

"Ye shall not go after other gods, of the gods of the people which *are* around about you; (For the LORD thy God *is* a jealous God among you) lest the anger of the LORD thy God be kindled against thee, and destroy thee from off the face of the earth."
(Deuteronomy 6:14–15)

Comment: We are so very blessed that we are on the other side of the death and resurrection of our

Lord and Savior, Jesus. We have the documentation of the New Testament where our God gave His only begotten Son, to the death, to pay for our sins and salvation. No other god has done so much to save His chosen people. There is no other god with that power or ability.

The Second Commandment

II "Thou shalt not make unto thee any graven image, or any likeness *of any thing* that *is* in heaven above, or that *is* in the earth beneath, or that *is* in the water under the earth: Thou shalt not bow down thyself to them, nor serve them: for I the LORD thy God *am* a jealous God, visiting the iniquity of the fathers upon the children unto the third and fourth *generation* of them that hate Me; And showing mercy unto thousands of them that love Me, and keep My commandments."

(Exodus 20:4–6)

"And in all *things* that I have said unto you be circumspect: and make no mention of the name of other gods, neither let it be heard out of thy mouth."

(Exodus 23:13)

"Thou shalt make thee no molten gods."

(Exodus 34:17)

"Ye shall make you no idols nor graven image, neither rear you up a standing image, neither shall ye set up *any* image of stone in your land, to bow down unto it: for I *am* the LORD your God."

(Leviticus 26:1)

"Take ye therefore good heed unto yourselves; for ye saw no manner of similitude on the day *that* the LORD spake unto you in Ho'reb out of the midst of the fire: Lest ye corrupt *yourselves*, and make you a graven image, the similitude of figure, the likeness of male or female, The likeness of any beast that *is* on the earth, the likeness of any any winged fowl that flieth in the air, The likeness of any thing that creepeth on the ground, the likeness of any fish that *is* in the waters beneath the earth: And lest thou lift up thine eyes unto heaven, and when thou seest the sun, and the moon, and the stars, *even* all the host of heaven, shouldest be driven to worship them, and serve them, which the LORD thy God hath divided unto all nations under the whole heaven."

(Deuteronomy 4:15–19)

"(For ye know how we have dwelt in the land of E'gypt; and how we came through the nations which ye passed by; And ye have seen their abomination,

and their idols, wood and stone, silver
and gold, which *were* among them:)"
(Deuteronomy 29:16–17)

Comment: Not to put the cart before the horse, but in the fourth commandment, we find that God is the creator of all things. This being the case, how can we take anything He has already made and turn it into a god and worship it? Can anything we make out of wood or stone send rain if we ask it? Do you think a statue or idol really loves you?

God loves us and tells us so in the second commandment. He is a jealous God. If He were not jealous, then we would not matter to Him. But we do matter because He loves us more than any other thing that He created. Not only does He love us, but He also wants us to love Him. He tells us in Exodus 20:6 how to love Him when He says: "And showing mercy unto thousands of them that love Me and keep My commandments."

Today, many Christians collect angels, crosses, statutes of different saints, and of course, statues of Jesus on a cross. I am not sure the Lord wants us to do these things, as I cannot find any scripture asking or telling us to do so. In fact, that is what the second commandment is all about. I think one reason for this instruction is that by having a statute in your home and praying toward it implies to the very young that may be living or visiting with you that the statue is your God. If God had wanted to give us an image of Himself, He would have done so. Today, we are very self-centered; we use our cell phones to take pictures of ourselves called "selfies." With God, it is different. No man has seen God except the Son. A man once asked to see God on Mount Sinai, where the commandments were given.

In Exodus 33:18, Moses asked God to let him see Him.

> "And he said, I beseech Thee, show me Thy glory. And He said, I will make all My goodness pass before thee, and I will proclaim the name of the LORD before thee; and will be gracious to whom I will be gracious, and will show mercy on whom I will show mercy. And He said, Thou canst not see My face: for there shall no man see Me, and live. And the LORD said, Behold, *there is* a place by Me, and thou shalt stand upon a rock: And it shall come to pass, while My glory passeth by, that I will put thee in a clift of the rock, and will cover thee with My hand while I pass by: And I will take away Mine hand, and thou shalt see My back parts: but My face shall not be seen."
>
> (Exodus 33:18–23)

Let us look at it a different way. Suppose Moses had seen the face of God. Would it have changed anything? Yes, indeed! Moses would have died on the spot as the scripture says.

We will see God face-to-face in due time, in His time. When He returns, we will all see Him. Between now and then, we should prepare ourselves for that meeting by learning and keeping all of his commandments and precepts.

A young, expectant daughter once told her father that she had never been so excited to meet someone, meaning her new child. That is how it should be with all Christians, eagerly waiting to see Jesus. Just like Moses, we should want to see Him, to meet Him, to embrace Him, and to tell Him that we love Him, face-to-face. This is certainly not against the scriptures.

"Seek the LORD and His strength, seek His face continually."
(1 Chronicles 16:11)

"This *is* the generation of them that seek Him, that seek Thy face, O Ja'cob. Se'lah."
(Psalm 24:6)

"*When Thou saidst,* Seek ye my face; my heart said unto Thee, Thy face, LORD, will I seek."
(Psalm 27:8)

"Seek the LORD, and His strength: seek His face evermore."
(Psalm 105.4)

The Third Commandment

III **"Thou shalt not take the name of the LORD thy God in vain; for the LORD will not hold him guiltless that taketh His name in vain."**

(Exodus 20:7)

"And ye shall not swear by My name falsely, neither shalt thou profane the name of thy God: I am the LORD.*"*

(Leviticus 19:12)

"Thou shalt fear the LORD thy God, and serve Him, and shalt swear by His name."

(Deuteronomy 6:13)

"Thou shalt fear the LORD thy God; him shalt thou serve, and to Him shalt thou cleave, and swear by His name."

(Deuteronomy 10:20)

Comment: There is no record of any thing the Lord has done that is wrong. Even the great flood that covered the earth in the days of Noah was a good thing. It was a cleansing and a new start for humanity. Therefore, all that he has done is right and good. He never sinned. He set the example for us to live by. Every time Jesus, the Son, spoke of God, the Father, He did it with honor and glory to the Father. How can we expect His forgiveness if we wrongfully and shamefully use His name?

The Fourth Commandment

IV "Remember the sabbath day, to keep it holy. Six days shalt thou labour, and do all thy work: But the seventh day *is* the sabbath of the LORD thy God: *in it* thou shalt not do any work, thou, nor thy son, nor thy daughter, thy manservant, nor thy maidservant, nor thy cattle, nor thy stranger that *is* within thy gates: For *in* six days the LORD made heaven and earth, the sea, and all that in them *is*, and rested the seventh day: wherefore the LORD blessed the sabbath day, and hallowed it."

(Exodus 20:8–11)

"And God blessed the seventh day, and sanctified it: because that in it He had rested from all His work which God created and made."

(Genesis 2:3)

"And he said unto them, This *is that* which the LORD hath said, Tomorrow *is* the rest of the holy sabbath unto the LORD: bake *that* which ye will bake *to day*, and seethe that ye will seethe; and that which remaineth over lay up for you to be kept until the morning."

(Exodus 16:23)

"Six days thou shalt do thy work, and on the seventh day thou shalt rest: that thine ox and thine ass may rest, and the son of thy handmaid, and the stranger, may be refreshed."

(Exodus 23:12)

"And the LORD spake unto Mo'ses, saying, Speak thou also unto the children of Is'ra-el, saying, Verily My sabbaths ye shall keep: for it *is* a sign between Me and you throughout your generations; that *ye* may know that I *am* the LORD that doth sanctify you. Ye shall keep the sabbath therefore; for it *is* holy unto you: every one that defileth it shall surely be put to death: for whosoever doeth *any* work therein, that soul shall be cut off from among his people. Six days may work be done; but in the seventh *is* the sabbath of rest, holy to the LORD: whosoever doeth *any* work in the sabbath day, he shall surely be put to death. Wherefore the children of Is'ra-el shall keep the sabbath, to observe the sabbath throughout their generations, *for* a perpetual covenant. It *is* a sign between Me and the children of Is'ra-el forever: for *in six* days the LORD made heaven and earth, and on the seventh day He rested, and was refreshed."

(Exodus 31:12–17)

"Six days thou shalt work, but the seventh day thou shalt rest: in earing time and in harvest thou shalt rest."
(Exodus 34:21)

"Keep the sabbath day to sanctify it, as the LORD thy God hath commanded thee. Six days thou shalt labor, and do all thy work: But the seventh day *is* the sabbath of the LORD thy God: *in it* thou shalt not do any work, thou, nor thy son, nor thy daughter, nor thy manservant, nor thy maidservant, nor thine ox, nor thine ass, nor any of thy cattle, nor thy stranger that *is* within thy gates; that thy manservant and thy maidservant may rest as well as thou."
(Deuteronomy 5:12–14)

"Thus saith the LORD; Take heed to yourselves, and bear no burden on the sabbath day, nor bring *it* in by the gates of Je-ru'sa-lem; Neither carry forth a burden out of your houses on the sabbath day, neither do ye any work, but hallow ye the sabbath day, as I commanded your fathers."
(Jeremiah 17:21–22)

Comment: This commandment is very special to God. He tells us to remember the sabbath day because He does not want us to ever forget it. It is the only commandment we are told to remember. We are told to keep it holy. Just as God wants us to be holy, we also need to keep the sabbath day holy. This is accomplished by keeping it separate from all other days and not doing any work on it. It is a day of rest from working in our trade or business. Rest is what it was created for. After God worked on creation for six days, He rested on the seventh day, which He called the sabbath day. We are told to do just as God did, by doing our labor and all our work in six days. But the seventh day is the sabbath of the Lord thy God and in it, we shall not do any work. It is a gift from God, a day of rest. However, there are exceptions as Jesus explained in Mark 3:4 and Luke 6:9.

Jesus asked in Mark 3:4, "Is it lawful to do good on the sabbath days, or to do evil? to save life, or to kill?"

Luke 6:9 reads, "Then said Je'sus unto them, I will ask you one thing; Is it lawful on the sabbath days to do good, or to do evil? to save life, or to destroy *it*?"

Yes, there is work that is necessary to save and protect life on the sabbath day. Police and firefighters are necessary to respond to emergencies. Military assignments around the world require 24-7 availability. EMTs, nurses, and doctors in emergency rooms are there to save lives on the sabbath day. This is necessary and acceptable work on the sabbath day, and it also applies to health care providers for the elderly.

Not only are we responsible for our families not working on the sabbath day, but we are also responsible for others. It is the same thing where you would never consider aiding and abetting someone in a murder, because it is a sin to kill. The fourth commandment clearly tells us we are responsible for the stranger that is within our gates. This stranger could be a distant relative visiting for a few days. It is our obligation to protect them from breaking the fourth commandment by not allowing them to work on the sabbath day. As long as anyone is under our roof, we are obligated to protect them from sinning just as we are responsible for protecting them from any other danger that might come upon them.

Let's take this a step further. On the way home from church on the sabbath day, you stop by and get gas because you are down to a quarter of a tank. Or you stop by the hardware store to pick up a lawn rake to replace the one you broke the week before. Or after church, you take your family to a nearby restaurant and enjoy a fine dinner. Notice that none of these things are life-threatening, critical, or urgent. All of those facilities should likewise be observing the same sabbath day by not working or being open for business. Giving them your business on the sabbath day causes them to stay open and hire employees to also break the fourth commandment. Buying and selling on the sabbath day is breaking the fourth commandment. That is why the day before the sabbath is called the day of preparation. It is a day to wrap up loose ends beforehand and get ready for the sabbath day.

Nehemiah led the third group of Jews back to Jerusalem after their captivity in Babylon. While rebuilding the wall to the city, he observed people trying to buy and sell on the sabbath day.

"In those days saw I in Ju'dah *some* treading wine presses on the sabbath, and bringing in sheaves, and lading asses; as also wine, grapes, and figs, and all *manner of* burdens, which they brought into Je-ru'sa-lem on the sabbath day: and I testified *against them* in the day wherein they sold victuals. There dwelt men of Tyre also therein, which brought fish, and all manner of ware, and sold on the sabbath unto the children of Ju'dah, and in Je-ru'sa-lem. Then I contended with the nobles of Ju'dah, and said unto them, What evil thing *is* this that ye do, and profane the sabbath day? Did not your fathers thus, and did not our God bring all this evil upon us, and upon this city? yet ye bring more wrath upon Is'rael by profaning the sabbath. And it came to pass, that when the gates of Je-ru'sa-lem began to be dark before the sabbath, I command that the gates should be shut, and charged that they should not be opened till after the sabbath: and *some* of my servants set I at the gates, *that* there should no burden be brought in on the sabbath day. So the merchants and sellers of all kind of ware lodged without Je-ru'sa-lem once or twice. Then I testified against them, and said unto them, Why lodge ye about the wall? If you do *so* again I will lay hands on you. From that time forth came they no *more* on the sabbath. And I commanded the Le'vites that they should cleanse themselves, and *that* they should come *and* keep the gates, to sanctify the sabbath day."

(Nehemiah 13:15–22)

This is another precept for protecting the fourth commandment, keeping the sabbath holy.

So what was created in the fourth commandment and yet never mentioned. Six days shalt thou labor and do all thy work; but the seventh day is the sabbath of the LORD thy God. In the beginning, the first seven days became the week, but it was not mentioned as such in the scriptures. It is another way God has given us to measure time. He created the sun, which the earth rotates around once and measures a year, just as He created the moon, which rotates around the earth and gives us the months. So it is the sun and moon we use to measure the time of our years and months. But the week itself, a measure of seven days, was created by God within the fourth commandment. It is expressed again in the book of Genesis where Jacob wants to marry Rachel. He agrees to work for Laban, her father, for seven years. Notice how it is expressed.

"Fulfil her week, and we will give thee this also for the service which thou shalt serve with me yet seven other years."

(Genesis 29:27)

> "And Ja'cob did so, and fulfilled her week: and he gave him Ra'chel his daughter to wife also."
>
> (Genesis 29:28)

There is a division among most Christians today as to which day the true sabbath is. Some say Sunday is the sabbath while others profess Saturday to be the true sabbath day. Many say it does not matter which day we worship the Lord as long as it is one day each week. How can this be? Division? God is not divided and clearly states that the seventh day is the sabbath of the Lord thy God. No matter what we say or conclude, we cannot change the day which the Lord has set for *His* sabbath day. Read the fourth commandment again; it clearly states: "But the seventh day *is* the sabbath of the LORD thy God:" (Exodus 20:10). It cannot be more clear than that.

We need not quibble nor be divided over a commandment that God gave us. The King James Bible gives us more direction concerning the commandments.

> "Ye shall not add unto the word which I command you, neither shall ye diminish *ought* from it, that ye may keep the commandments of the LORD your God which I command you."
>
> (Deuteronomy 4:2)

> "What thing soever I command you, observe to do it: thou shalt not add thereto, nor diminish from it."
> (Deuteronomy 12:32)

> "Add thou not unto His words, lest He reprove thee, and thou be found a liar."
> (Proverbs 30:6)

Jesus talked about this in the New Testament:

> "For verily I say unto you, Till heaven and earth pass, one jot or one tittle shall in no wise pass from the law, till all be fulfilled."
> (Matthew 5:18)

So what do you do if you are not sure? Both days cannot be correct. One is right, and the other is wrong. One is true, and the other is false. Remembering the truth can set you free, you must find it. Pray to the Lord for understanding and spiritual wisdom. Ask Him to lead you to His truth, that you might be better to do His will and obey all of His commandments. Once again, Jesus instructs us:

> "Ask, and it shall be given you; seek, and ye shall find; knock, and it shall be opened unto you."
> (Matthew 7:7)

The Fifth Commandment

V **"Honor thy father and thy mother: that thy days may be long upon the land which the LORD thy God giveth thee."**

(Exodus 20:12)

"Ye shall fear every man his mother, and his father, and keep My sabbaths:"
(Leviticus 19:3)

"Honor thy father and thy mother, as the LORD thy God hath commanded thee; that thy days may be prolonged, and that it may go well with thee, in the land which the LORD thy God giveth thee."

(Deuteronomy 5:16)

"Ye shall fear every man his mother, and his father, and keep My sabbaths: I am the Lord your God."

(Leviticus 19:3)

"For God commanded, saying, Honor thy Father and mother: and, He that curseth father or mother, let him die the death. But ye say, Whosoever shall say to *his* father or *his* mother, *It is* a gift, by whatsoever thou mightest be profited by me; And honor not his father or his mother, *he shall be free.* Thus have ye made the commandment of God of none effect by your tradition. Ye hypocrites, well did I-sa'iah prophesy of you saying. This people draweth near unto Me with their mouth, and honoreth Me with *their lips*; but their heart is far from Me. But in vain they do worship Me teaching *for* doctrines the commandments of men."

(Matthew 15:4–9)

"For Mo'ses said, Honor thy father and thy mother; and, Whoso curseth father or mother; let him die the death: But ye say, If a man shall say to his father or mother, *It is* Corban, that is to say, a gift, by whatsoever thou mightest be profited by me; *he shall be free*. And ye suffer him no more to do ought for his father or his mother; Making the word of God of none effect through your tradition, which ye have delivered: and many such like things do ye."

(Mark 7:10–13)

"Children, obey your parents in the LORD: for this is right. Honor thy father and mother; (which is the first commandment with promise;) That it may be well with thee, and thou mayest live long on the earth."

(Ephesians 6:1–3)

"Children, obey *your* parents in all things: for this is well pleasing unto the Lord."

(Colossians 3:20)

Comment: The last thing that God created was a man and a woman, reflections of His very image. And we were so blessed from the very beginning. All that God created was made before us so that everything was there for us to enjoy, including the beautiful garden provided for Adam and Eve. And after God created us, *He gave us His very first precept* which reads:

And God blessed them, and God said unto them, *"Be fruitful, and multiply,* and replenish the earth, and subdue it: and have dominion over the fish of the sea, and over the fowl of the air, and over every living thing that moveth upon the earth."

(Genesis 1:28 Emphasis mine)

Think about what God just said: "Be fruitful and multiply, and replenish the earth." He did not just make a man and a woman, He made a father and a mother. He told them to be fruitful and multiply, to be parents. He honors them for doing so in the fifth commandment. Notice please that there is no mention by God to abort our children. The precept is: "Be fruitful and multiply."

In this day and age, we have men with men and women with women, living together and even marrying. This is abomination to the Lord and is so stated in the following books of Leviticus, Romans, and Colossians.

> Thou shalt not lie with mankind, as with woman kind: it *is* abomination.
> (Leviticus 18:22)

> If a man also lie with mankind, as he lieth with a women, both of them have committed an abomination: they shall surely be put to death; their blood *shall be* upon them.
> (Leviticus 20:13)

"And likewise also the men, leaving the natural use of the woman, burned in their lust one toward another; men with men working that which is unseemly, and receiving in themselves that recompence of their error which was meet."
(Romans 1:27)

"Know ye not that the unrighteous shall not inherit the kingdom of God? Be not deceived: neither fornicators, nor idolaters, nor adulterers, nor effeminate, nor abusers of themselves with mankind, Nor thieves, nor covetous, nor drunkards, nor revilers, nor extortioners, shall inherit the kingdom of God."
(1 Corinthians 6:9–10)

Men with men and woman with woman cannot fulfill that very first precept of God; to be fruitful and multiply. They cannot reproduce children to help defend a nation in time of war. Since they are unable to reproduce and perpetuate their existence, they need to persuade or entice others to join their ranks. They are as dead trees unable to bear fruit.

Another interesting point about the fifth commandment is that it is the commandment that dates when the Ten Commandments were given. The commandments were given at Mount Sinai while the Hebrews were still in the wilderness, before they entered the promised land.

The Sixth Commandment

VI **"Thou shalt not kill."** (Exodus 20:13)

"And Cain talked with A'bel his brother: and it came to pass, when they were in the field, that Cain rose up against A'bel his brother, and slew him. And the LORD said unto Cain, Where *is* A'bel thy brother? And he said, I know not: *Am* I my brother's keeper? And He said, What hast thou done? the voice of thy brother's blood crieth unto Me from the ground. And now *art* thou cursed from the earth, which hath opened her mouth to receive thy brother's blood from thy hand; When thou tillest the ground, it shall not henceforth yield unto thee her strength; a fugitive and a vagabond shalt thou be in the earth."

(Genesis 4:8–12)

"And He said unto him, Why callest thou Me good? *there is* none good but one, *that is*, God: but if thou wilt enter into life, keep the commandments. He saith unto Him, Which? Je'sus said, thou shalt do no murder, thou shalt not commit adultery, thou shalt not steal, thou shalt not bear false witness."

(Matthew 19:17–18)

"Ye have heard that it was said by them of old time, thou shalt not kill; and whoso ever shall kill shall be in danger of the judgement: But I say unto you, That whosoever is angry with his brother without a cause shall be in danger of the judgement: and whosoever shall say to his brother, Raca, shall be in danger of the council: but whosoever shall say, thou fool, shall be in danger of hell fire."

(Matthew 5:21–22)

Comment: This commandment is straightforward, especially if you are watching a murder mystery on television. Murder is wrong, sinful, and violates the sixth commandment. However, there are exceptions for killing another person. Notice how in Matthew 19:18 Jesus told the rich man not to commit murder. He did not say not to kill, but not to commit murder.

Self-defense is a perfect example. This is what happens when one nation attacks another nation. Returning fire is an act of self-defense. There are dozens of examples of people carrying a weapon into a movie theater and opening fire on innocent people. This person is certainly violating the sixth commandment and must be justly stopped using equal force. Another example of justifiable killing is called capital punishment. An individual found guilty of willfully killing another person is judged and sentenced to death or imprisonment. In cases of the accidental death of another person, God understands how this might happen and provides His solution in the books of Numbers and Deuteronomy.

> "And the LORD spake unto Mo'ses, saying, Speak unto the children of Is'ra-el, and say unto them, When ye come over Jor'don into the land of Ca'naan; Then ye shall appoint you cities to be cities of refuge for you; that the slayer may flee thither, which killeth any person at unawares. And they shall be unto you cities for refuge from the avenger; that the manslayer die not, until he stand before the congregation in judgement."
> (Numbers 35:9–12)

> "As when a man goeth into the wood with his neighbor to hew wood, and his hand brought a stroke with the ax to cut down the tree, and the head slippeth from the helve, and lighteth

upon his neighbor, that he die; he shall flee unto one of those cities, and live."
(Deuteronomy 19:5)

The Seventh Commandment

VII **"Thou shalt not commit adultery."**
(Exodus 20:14)

"And the man that committeth adultery with *another* man's wife, *even he* that committeth adultery with his neighbor's wife, the adulterer and the adulteress shall surely be put to death."
(Leviticus 20:10)

"Ye have heard that it was said by them of old time, Thou shalt not commit adultery: But I say unto you, That whosoever looketh on a women to lust after her hath committed adultery with her already in his heart."
(Matthew 5:27–28)

"Neither shalt thou commit adultery."
(Deuteronomy 5:18)

"He saith unto Him, Which? Je'sus said, thou shalt do no murder, thou shalt not commit adultery, thou shalt not steal, thou shalt not bear false witness,"
(Matthew 19:18)

> "Thou knowest the commandments, Do not commit adultery,…"
>
> (Mark 10:19)

> "For this, Thou shall not commit adultery, Thou shalt not kill."
>
> (Romans 13:9)

> "For He that said, Do not commit adultery, said also, Do not kill."
>
> (James 2:11)

Comment: This is the only commandment that requires at least two people to physically violate it. It involves a married person having intercourse with another person they are not married to. The laws of man have drifted far from the seventh commandment of our God. There are some countries around the world where the act of adultery is not illegal. In the United States, laws about adultery vary greatly. In the state of Maryland, adultery is a misdemeanor punishable by a fine of ten dollars. This is the website from which this fact was taken: http://wtop.com/maryland/2018/02/md-lawmakers-consider-decriminalizing-adultery/

The Eighth Commandment

VIII *"Thou shalt not steal."*

(Exodus 20:15)

> "Ye shall not steal, neither deal falsely, neither lie one to another."
>
> (Leviticus 19:11)

"He saith unto Him, Which? Je'sus said, thou shall do no murder, thou shall not commit adultery, thou shalt not steal,…"

(Matthew 19:18)

"Thou knowest the commandments, Do not commit adultery, Do not kill, Do not steal,…"

(Mark 10:19)

"For this, Thou shalt not commit adultery, Thou shalt not kill, Thou shalt not steal,…"

(Romans 13:9)

"Let him that stole steal no more: but rather let him labor, working with *his* hands the thing which is good, that he may have to give to him that needeth."

(Ephesians 4:28)

Comment: As Christians, we are to give freely, lend freely, and share freely. We are not to take anything that is not our own from another person.

The Ninth Commandment

IX "Thou shalt not bear false witness against thy neighbor."

(Exodus 20:16)

"Thou shalt not raise a false report: put not thine hand with the wicked to be an unrighteous witness."

(Exodus 23:1)

"Whoso killeth any person, the murder shall be put to death by the mouth of witnesses: but one witness shall not testify against any person *to cause him* to die."

(Numbers 35:30)

"At the mouth of two witnesses, or three witnesses, shall he that is worthy of death be put to death; *but* at the mouth of one witness he shall not be put to death."

(Deuteronomy 17:6)

"One witness shall not rise up against a man for any iniquity, or for any sin, in any sin that he sinneth: at the mouth of two witnesses, or at the mouth of three witnesses, shall the matter be established. If a false witness rise up against any man to testify against him *that which* is wrong; Then both the men, between whom the controversy *is*, shall stand before the LORD, before the priests and judges, which shall be in those days; And the judges shall make diligent inquisition: and, behold, *if* the witness *be* a false witness, and hath tes-

tified falsely against his brother; Then shall ye do unto him, as he had thought to have done unto his brother: so shalt thou put the evil away from among you."
(Deuteronomy 19:15–19)

"Deliver me not over unto the will of mine enemies: for false witnesses are risen up against me, and such as breathe out cruelty."
(Psalm 27:12)

"False witnesses did rise up; they laid to my charge *things* that I knew not."
(Psalm 35:11)

"But if he will not hear *thee, then* take with thee one or two more, that in the mouth of two or three witnesses every word may be established."
(Matthew 18:16)

"He saith unto Him, Which? Je'sus said, thou shalt do no murder, thou shalt not commit adultery, thou shalt not steal, thou shalt not bear false witness,…"
(Matthew 19:18)

"Ye are of *your* father the devil, and the lust of your father ye will do. He was a murderer from the beginning, and abode not in the truth, because there is no truth in him. When he speaketh a lie,

he speaketh of his own: for he is a liar, and the father of it."
(John 8:44)

"This *is* the third *time* I am coming to you. In the mouth of two or three witnesses shall every word be established."
(2 Corinthians 13:1)

The Tenth Commandment

X **"Thou shalt not covet thy neighbor's house, thou shalt not covet they neighbor's wife, nor his manservant, nor his maidservant, nor his ox, nor his ass, nor anything that *is* thy neighbor's."**
(Exodus 20:17)

"Neither shalt thou desire thy neighbor's wife, neither shalt thou covet thy neighbor's house, his field, or his manservant, or his maidservant, his ox, or his ass, or any *thing* that *is* thy neighbor's."
(Deuteronomy 5:21)

"What shall we say then? *Is* the law sin? God forbid. Nay, I had not known sin, but by the law: for I had not known lust, except the law had said, Thou shalt not covet."
(Romans 7:7)

Comment: Reading the tenth commandment might cause one to think the Lord does not want us to have a house, wife, manservant, maidservant, ox, ass, or anything. Such is not the case. He wants us to be successful and prosperous from the works of our own hands. Coveting is an inordinate desire to possess what belongs to another, usually tangible things. Before someone steals from another person, they coveted what they stole. It is coveting another's man's wife that will lead to adultery. To have needs is normal, but to worry about what another person has to the point where you become resentful of any of their possessions is pure envy and leads to coveting.

THE PSALM OF ALL PSALMS

The Psalm of all Psalms is Psalm 119. It is the longest chapter in the entire King James Bible. The author is not known but thought to be Ezra the Priest. There are 1,189 chapters in the Bible. No other chapter compliments and praises God's statutes, precepts, and commandments more than Psalm 119. Enjoy.

Aleph

1. Blessed are the undefiled in the way, who walk in the law of the LORD.
2. Blessed are they that keep His testimonies, and that seek him with the whole heart.
3. They also do no iniquity, they walk in His ways.
4. Thou has commanded us to keep thy precepts diligently.
5. O that my ways were directed to keep his statutes.
6. Then shall I not be ashamed, when I have respect unto all thy commandments.
7. I will praise thee with uprightness of heart, when I shall have learned thy righteous judgements.
8. I will keep thy statutes: O forsake me not utterly.

Beth

9. Wherewithal shall a young man cleanse his way? by taking heed thereto according to thy word.
10. With my whole heart have I sought thee: O let me not wander from thy commandments.
11. Thy word have I hid in my heart, that I might not sin against thee.
12. Blessed art thou, O LORD: teach me thy statutes.
13. With my lips have I declared all thy judgements of thy mouth.
14. I have rejoiced in the way of thy testimonies, as much as in all riches.
15. I will meditate in thy precepts, and have respect unto thy ways.
16. I will delight myself in thy statutes: I will not forget thy word.

Gimel

17. Deal bountifully with thy servant, that I may live, and keep thy word.
18. Open thou mine eyes, that I may behold wondrous things out of thy law.
19. I am a stranger in the earth: hide not thy commandments from me.
20. My soul breaketh for the longing that it hath unto thy judgments at all times.
21. Thou hast rebuked the proud that are cursed, which do err from thy commandments.
22. Remove from me reproach and contempt; for I have kept thy testimonies.

23. Princes also did sit and speak against me: but thy servant did meditate in thy statutes.
24. Thy testimonies also are my delight and my counsellors.

Daleth

25. My soul cleaveth unto the dust: quicken thou me according to thy word.
26. I have declared my ways, and thou heardest me: teach me thy statutes.
27. Make me to understand the way of thy precepts: so shall I talk of thy wondrous works.
28. My soul melteth for heaviness: strengthen thou me according unto thy word.
29. Remove from me the way of lying: and grant me thy law graciously.
30. I have chosen the way of truth: thy judgments have I laid before me.
31. I have stuck unto thy testimonies: O LORD, put me not to shame.
32. I will run the way of thy commandments, when thou shalt enlarge my heart.

He

33. Teach me, O LORD, the way of thy statutes; and I shall keep it unto the end.
34. Give me understanding, and I shall keep thy law; yea, I shall observe it with my whole heart.
35. Make me to go in the path of thy commandments; for therein do I delight.
36. Incline my heart unto thy testimonies, and not to covetousness.

37. Turn away mine eyes from beholding vanity; and quicken thou me in thy way.
38. Stablish thy word unto thy servant, who is devoted to thy fear.
39. Turn away my reproach which I fear: for thy judgments are good.
40. Behold, I have longed after thy precepts: quicken me in thy righteousness.

Vau

41. Let thy mercies come also unto me, O LORD, even thy salvation, according to thy word.
42. So shall I have wherewith to answer him that reproacheth me: for I trust in thy word.
43. And take not the word of truth utterly out of my mouth; for I have hoped in thy judgments.
44. So shall I keep thy law continually for ever and ever.
45. And I will walk at liberty: for I seek thy precepts.
46. I will speak of thy testimonies also before kings, and will not be ashamed.
47. And I will delight myself in thy commandments, which I have loved.
48. My hands also will I lift up unto thy commandments, which I have loved; and I will meditate in thy statutes.

Zain

49. Remember the word unto thy servant, upon which thou hast caused me to hope.
50. This is my comfort in my affliction: for thy word hath quickened me.

51. The proud have had me greatly in derision: yet have I not declined from thy law.
52. I remembered thy judgments of old, O LORD; and have comforted myself.
53. Horror hath taken hold upon me because of the wicked that forsake thy law.
54. Thy statutes have been my songs in the house of my pilgrimage.
55. I have remembered thy name, O LORD, in the night, and have kept thy law.
56. This I had, because I kept thy precepts.

Cheth

57. Thou art my portion, O LORD: I have said that I would keep thy words.
58. I intreated thy favour with my whole heart: be merciful unto me according to thy word.
59. I thought on my ways, and turned my feet unto thy testimonies.
60. I made haste, and delayed not to keep thy commandments.
61. The bands of the wicked have robbed me: but I have not forgotten thy law.
62. At midnight I will rise to give thanks unto thee because of thy righteous judgments.
63. I am a companion of all them that fear thee, and of them that keep thy precepts.
64. The earth, O LORD, is full of thy mercy: teach me thy statutes.

Teth

65. Thou hast dealt well with thy servant, O LORD, according unto thy word.
66. Teach me good judgment and knowledge: for I have believed thy commandments.
67. Before I was afflicted I went astray: but now have I kept thy word.
68. Thou art good, and doest good; teach me thy statutes.
69. The proud have forged a lie against me: but I will keep thy precepts with my whole heart.
70. Their heart is as fat as grease; but I delight in thy law.
71. It is good for me that I have been afflicted; that I might learn thy statutes.
72. The law of thy mouth is better unto me than thousands of gold and silver.

Jod

73. Thy hands have made me and fashioned me: give me understanding, that I may learn thy commandments.
74. They that fear thee will be glad when they see me; because I have hoped in thy word.
75. I know, O LORD, that thy judgments are right, and that thou in faithfulness hast afflicted me.
76. Let, I pray thee, thy merciful kindness be for my comfort, according to thy word unto thy servant.
77. Let thy tender mercies come unto me, that I may live: for thy law is my delight.
78. Let the proud be ashamed; for they dealt perversely with me without a cause: but I will meditate in thy precepts.
79. Let those that fear thee turn unto me, and those that have known thy testimonies.

80. Let my heart be sound in thy statutes; that I be not ashamed.

Caph

81. My soul fainteth for thy salvation: but I hope in thy word.
82. Mine eyes fail for thy word, saying, When wilt thou comfort me?
83. For I am become like a bottle in the smoke; yet do I not forget thy statutes.
84. How many are the days of thy servant? when wilt thou execute judgment on them that persecute me?
85. The proud have digged pits for me, which are not after thy law.
86. All thy commandments are faithful: they persecute me wrongfully; help thou me.
87. They had almost consumed me upon earth; but I forsook not thy precepts.
88. Quicken me after thy lovingkindness; so shall I keep the testimony of thy mouth.

Lamed

89. For ever, O LORD, thy word is settled in heaven.
90. Thy faithfulness is unto all generations: thou hast established the earth, and it abideth.
91. They continue this day according to thine ordinances: for all are thy servants.
92. Unless thy law had been my delights, I should then have perished in mine affliction.
93. I will never forget thy precepts: for with them thou hast quickened me.
94. I am thine, save me; for I have sought thy precepts.

95. The wicked have waited for me to destroy me: but I will consider thy testimonies.
96. I have seen an end of all perfection: but thy commandment is exceeding broad.

Mem

97. O how love I thy law! it is my meditation all the day.
98. Thou through thy commandments hast made me wiser than mine enemies: for they are ever with me.
99. I have more understanding than all my teachers: for thy testimonies are my meditation.
100. I understand more than the ancients, because I keep thy precepts.
101. I have refrained my feet from every evil way, that I might keep thy word.
102. I have not departed from thy judgments: for thou hast taught me.
103. How sweet are thy words unto my taste! yea, sweeter than honey to my mouth!
104. Through thy precepts I get understanding: therefore I hate every false way.

Nun

105. Thy word is a lamp unto my feet, and a light unto my path.
106. I have sworn, and I will perform it, that I will keep thy righteous judgments.
107. I am afflicted very much: quicken me, O LORD, according unto thy word.
108. Accept, I beseech thee, the freewill offerings of my mouth, O LORD, and teach me thy judgments.

109. My soul is continually in my hand: yet do I not forget thy law.
110. The wicked have laid a snare for me: yet I erred not from thy precepts.
111. Thy testimonies have I taken as an heritage forever: for they are the rejoicing of my heart.
112. I have inclined mine heart to perform thy statutes alway, even unto the end.

Samech

113. I hate vain thoughts: but thy law do I love.
114. Thou art my hiding place and my shield: I hope in thy word.
115. Depart from me, ye evildoers: for I will keep the commandments of my God.
116. Uphold me according unto thy word, that I may live: and let me not be ashamed of my hope.
117. Hold thou me up, and I shall be safe: and I will have respect unto thy statutes continually.
118. Thou hast trodden down all them that err from thy statutes: for their deceit is falsehood.
119. Thou puttest away all the wicked of the earth like dross: therefore I love thy testimonies.
120. My flesh trembleth for fear of thee; and I am afraid of thy judgments.

Ain

121. I have done judgment and justice: leave me not to mine oppressors.
122. Be surety for thy servant for good: let not the proud oppress me.

123. Mine eyes fail for thy salvation, and for the word of thy righteousness.
124. Deal with thy servant according unto thy mercy, and teach me thy statutes.
125. I am thy servant; give me understanding, that I may know thy testimonies.
126. *It is* time for *Thee*, LORD, to work: for they have made void thy law.
127. Therefore I love thy commandments above gold; yea, above fine gold.
128. Therefore I esteem all thy precepts concerning all things to be right; and I hate every false way.

Pe

129. Thy testimonies are wonderful: therefore doth my soul keep them.
130. The entrance of thy words giveth light; it giveth understanding unto the simple.
131. I opened my mouth, and panted: for I longed for thy commandments.
132. Look thou upon me, and be merciful unto me, as thou usest to do unto those that love thy name.
133. Order my steps in thy word: and let not any iniquity have dominion over me.
134. Deliver me from the oppression of man: so will I keep thy precepts.
135. Make thy face to shine upon thy servant; and teach me thy statutes.
136. Rivers of waters run down mine eyes, because they keep not thy law.

Tzaddi

137. Righteous art thou, O LORD, and upright are thy judgments.
138. Thy testimonies that thou hast commanded are righteous and very faithful.
139. My zeal hath consumed me, because mine enemies have forgotten thy words.
140. Thy word is very pure: therefore thy servant loveth it.
141. I am small and despised: yet do not I forget thy precepts.
142. Thy righteousness is an everlasting righteousness, and thy law is the truth.
143. Trouble and anguish have taken hold on me: yet thy commandments are my delights.
144. The righteousness of thy testimonies is everlasting: give me understanding, and I shall live.

Koph

145. I cried with my whole heart; hear me, O LORD: I will keep thy statutes.
146. I cried unto thee; save me, and I shall keep thy testimonies.
147. I prevented the dawning of the morning, and cried: I hoped in thy word.
148. Mine eyes prevent the night watches, that I might meditate in thy word.
149. Hear my voice according unto thy lovingkindness: O LORD, quicken me according to thy judgment.
150. They draw nigh that follow after mischief: they are far from thy law.
151. Thou art near, O LORD; and all thy commandments are truth.

152. Concerning thy testimonies, I have known of old that thou hast founded them for ever.

Resh

153. Consider mine affliction, and deliver me: for I do not forget thy law.
154. Plead my cause, and deliver me: quicken me according to thy word.
155. Salvation is far from the wicked: for they seek not thy statutes.
156. Great are thy tender mercies, O LORD: quicken me according to thy judgments.
157. Many are my persecutors and mine enemies; yet do I not decline from thy testimonies.
158. I beheld the transgressors, and was grieved; because they kept not thy word.
159. Consider how I love thy precepts: quicken me, O LORD, according to thy loving kindness.
160. Thy word is true from the beginning: and every one of thy righteous judgments endureth forever.

Schin

161. Princes have persecuted me without a cause: but my heart standeth in awe of thy word.
162. I rejoice at thy word, as one that findeth great spoil.
163. I hate and abhor lying: but thy law do I love.
164. Seven times a day do I praise thee because of thy righteous judgments.
165. Great peace have they which love thy law: and nothing shall offend them.

166. LORD, I have hoped for thy salvation, and done thy commandments.
167. My soul hath kept thy testimonies; and I love them exceedingly.
168. I have kept thy precepts and thy testimonies: for all my ways are before thee.

Tau

169. Let my cry come near before thee, O LORD: give me understanding according to thy word.
170. Let my supplication come before thee: deliver me according to thy word.
171. My lips shall utter praise, when thou hast taught me thy statutes.
172. My tongue shall speak of thy word: for all thy commandments are righteousness.
173. Let thine hand help me; for I have chosen thy precepts.
174. I have longed for thy salvation, O LORD; and thy law is my delight.
175. Let my soul live, and it shall praise thee; and let thy judgements help me.
176. I have gone astray like a lost sheep; seek thy servant; for I do not forget thy commandments.

THE TWO GREATEST COMMANDMENTS

"Think not that I am come to destroy the law, or the prophets: I am not come to destroy, but to fulfill. For verily I say unto you, Till heaven and earth pass, one jot or one tittle shall in no wise pass from the law, till all be fulfilled. Whosoever therefore shall break one of these least commandments, and shall teach men so, he shall be called the least in the kingdom of heaven: but whosoever shall do and teach *them*, the same shall be called great in the kingdom of heaven."

(Matthew 5:17–19)

Our Lord and Savior Jesus is talking here. Notice that the Lord refers to the breaking of "one of these **least** commandments." What does that mean? Is one commandment greater than another? How is any commandment determined to be lesser, or greater than another? Look at Mark 12:29–31.

And Je'sus answered him, The first of all the commandments *is*, Hear, O Is'ra-el; The LORD our God is one LORD: And thou shalt love the Lord thy God with all thy heart, and with all thy soul, and with all thy mind, and with all thy strength: this *is* the first commandment. And the second *is* like, *namely* this, Thou shalt love thy neighbor as thyself. There is none other commandment greater than these.

Jesus tells us to first love God and then to love our neighbors. These are the greatest commandments. Consider that if we truly follow these two commands, we will not break the "lesser" commandments.

The *first great commandment* Jesus shared in Mark 12:29–30 *addressed loving God.* The first four of the Ten Commandments fall under this great commandment. They explain to us how we are to behave in order to not sin against the Lord.

> **THOU SHALT LOVE THE LORD THY GOD WITH ALL THY HEART, AND WITH ALL THY SOUL, AND WITH ALL THY MIND AND WITH ALL THY STRENGTH.**

The first of all the commandments is to love God.
The first four Commandments support this.

I   Thou shalt have no other gods before Me.

II Thou shalt not make unto thee any graven image, or any likeness *of any thing* that *is* in heaven above, or that *is* in the earth beneath, or that *is* in the water under the earth: Thou shalt not bow down thyself to them, nor serve them: for I the LORD thy God *am* a jealous God, visiting the iniquity of the fathers upon the children unto the third and fourth *generation* of them that hate Me; And showing mercy unto thousands of them that love Me, and keep My commandments.

III Thou shalt not take the name of the LORD thy God in vain; for the LORD will not hold him guiltless that taketh His name in vain.

IV Remember the sabbath day, to keep it holy. Six days shalt thou labour, and do all thy work: But the seventh day *is* the sabbath of the LORD thy God: *in it* thou shalt not do any work, thou, nor thy son, nor thy daughter, thy manservant, nor thy maidservant, nor thy cattle, nor thy stranger that *is* within thy gates: For *in* six days the LORD made heaven and earth, the sea, and all that in them *is,* and rested the seventh day: wherefore the LORD blessed the sabbath day, and hallowed it.

If we love Him, we will keep His commands.

The *second great commandment* Jesus shared in Mark 12:31 addressed loving people. The last six commandments fall under this command, as they explain how we are to live in peace and harmony without sinning against mankind.

THOU SHALT LOVE THY NEIGHBOR AS THYSELF.

V Honor thy father and thy mother: that thy days may be long upon the land which the LORD thy God giveth thee.

VI Thou shalt not kill.

VII Thou shalt not commit adultery.

VIII Thou shalt not steal.

IX Thou shalt not bear false witness against thy neighbor.

X Thou shalt not covet thy neighbor's house, thou shalt not covet thy neighbor's wife, nor his manservant, nor his maidservant, nor his ox, nor his ass, nor any thing that *is* thy neighbor's.

If we sincerely love our neighbor as we love ourselves, we will find ourselves honoring these commandments. Jesus intensifies this commandment in John 13:34, "A new commandment I give unto you, That ye love one another; as I have loved you, that ye also love one another." Now, we must love others as He loves us, not just as we love ourselves. Jesus set His standard of love high!

The greatest commandments require us to love. By fulfilling these, we are well on our way to keeping the others.

You have come a very long way in learning how to love the Lord by memorizing His Ten Commandments. I encourage you to also memorize these two new great commandments. You may use the chunking approach if needed.

His commandments are beautiful, what better place to hide them than in the safe repository of our hearts.

PURE RELIGION IN THE FIRST CHURCH

In the very early church, the apostles were met with furious opposition. They were thrown into prison and beaten, and yet they rejoiced that they were counted worthy to suffer shame for the name of the Lord Jesus. At the same time, there was an internal issue that had to be dealt with. The book of Acts reveals:

> And in those days, when the number of the disciples was multiplied, there arose a murmuring of the Gre'cians against the He'brews, because their widows were neglected in the daily ministration. Then the twelve called the multitude of the disciples unto them, and said, It is not reason that we should leave the word of God, and serve tables. Wherefore, brethren, look ye out among you seven men of honest report, full of the Ho'ly Ghost and wisdom, whom we may appoint over this business.
> (Acts 6:1–3)

Notice that the leaders of the church, the twelve apostles, including Matthias, delegated this responsibility to the disciples who were the ordinary church members just like us. After the apostles, this became the very first Christian group with an assigned mission. Notice also that at least thirteen years before the Book of Acts was written, James, the brother of Jesus, wrote the following in his book:

> Pure religion and undefiled before God and the Father is this, To visit the fatherless and widows in their affliction, and to keep himself unspotted from the world.
> (James 1:27)

Sometimes, in doing what we think is our spiritual business, we pass right by the widows and orphans. While we are so busy doing other good works like feeding the homeless, operating food pantries, building homes for Habitat for Humanity, etc., we go right past the widow's house without a thought of her. The life full of love and laughter she once had is gone, and she is left now all alone. Once willing and able to help others, she is no longer able to help herself. She makes difficult decisions every week, like whether to buy the can of tuna fish or to pay for needed medicines. They enter the sanctuary, some using canes or walkers. After the church services, they are last to leave as the younger people are much faster and beat them to their cars. The loneliness swells and follows her home to a place void of life and company. Cards, letters, and telephone calls are few. Living now on a very small fixed income, she forgoes small treats for herself so that she can give an offering to the Lord. The golden years get grayer every day. It seems there is no one who cares, and it is her prayers and faith in Jesus that sustain her.

PURE RELIGION IN THE CHURCH TODAY

After reading James 1:27, a solution was presented to a pastor in a small Maryland church. He concurred and shared the solution to the church board, which agreed to allow a new ministry to begin fifteen years ago in 2005. A contest was held to create a good name for this ministry, and the winning name chosen was

WONDERS, which is an acronym for:

Widows **O**rphans **N**ever **D**enied **E**verlasting **R**easonable **S**ervices.

Their official name and logo is:

✝ WONDERS ✝
Widows **O**rphans **N**ever **D**enied **E**verlasting **R**easonable **S**ervices, Inc.

"Pure religion and undefiled before God and the Father is this, To visit the fatherless and widows in their affliction, and to keep himself unspotted from the world." James 1:27

WONDERS has come a long way over the years. It has become a 501(c)(3) nonprofit corporation approved by the

IRS. With chapters in both Maryland and Florida, we continue to grow in support of widows and orphans.

Wanting to see such a ministry in every church, we invite all Christian churches to start a WONDERS chapter.

We do a lot of things to help widows, but this is the general procedure.

1. Each widow is taken to dinner and interviewed. A simple form entitled "Meet the Widow" is used to document their date of birth, address, telephone number, names of living children, list of medications, last eye exam, sizes of shoes and dresses, schools attended, work history, hobbies, health concerns, last visit to doctor/dentist, age of eyeglasses, favorite scripture, favorite meal, dessert, and emergency contact information.

2. We conduct a Wednesday afternoon Bible study for them that lasts about an hour and is followed by pastries and drinks. This keeps their weekends free and does not interfere with their Sabbath worship. We make sure each widow has a large print King James Bible. (This is also why we get their eyes examined and purchase new glasses if needed. You cannot read the Word if you cannot see it.)

   The Bible study is the key element for both WONDERS and the widows themselves. Here is what usually happens. Let's say you already have three widows in your group and a fourth one is invited to her first Bible study. The leader opens the study with a short prayer, and the widow sitting farthest from the new guest is asked to read two or three verses. The verses are briefly discussed for understanding, and the next widow is asked to read likewise. This is done to get everyone involved, including the newest widow. While this is coming to a conclusion, another member is preparing small treats for them at a table in another room. This is where God works WONDERS.

The four widows come to the table and are seated. After the blessing, the WONDERS members leave the widows alone. Here is what usually happens when a new widow is introduced to the group. The new widow will hardly say a word. She does not yet feel comfortable nor a part of the group. Her answers are very brief. They chitchat and are taken home until the following Wednesday.

After the scripture readings of the second Bible study, the ladies again head for the table of light refreshments, and the WONDERS members leave the room. The newest widow is a little more comfortable in the group, wearing a slightly wider smile but still answers with few words. She is certainly not bold enough to start a conversation. She does seem to be paying more attention to what is being said. During this visit, she may loosen up, greeting each person, and afterward, bidding each farewell.

At the third study, we notice the newest widow giving longer replies. She may share how she got her new blouse at Walmart, compliment another widow's appearance, and convey how glad she is to be with them. She may even bring up the subject of her husband's passing.

All that needs to be done by the WONDERS members at the fourth meeting is to lead the Bible study, prepare the refreshment table, and get out of the way. Chitter-chatter, *blab, blab*… You probably could not get a word in edgewise.

Four weeks ago, there was a widow who was alone. She is not alone now. Four weeks ago, she had no family. She has a family now. Four weeks ago, no one could understand what it really means to lose your husband. She has someone that understands now. Four weeks ago, she felt low and down in the dumps. Her self-esteem has risen. She felt all alone in her situation, with no one to talk to. Now she has the telephone numbers of three new widow friends she can call and talk to. Today, she has three new sisters who all can relate to her circumstances. She is no longer alone; she now belongs to a group and is a member of the team. A greater feeling of self-worth comes alive. Thank you, Father.

This is another example of leading the horse to water to make him thirsty. You set it all up, but it is the Holy Spirit that makes the horse drink. He causes the coarse burr of the widow's shyness to be smoothed down so that all the pieces can smoothly fit together. It is He, who transforms those who once felt they could not contribute to a greater cause into an uplifting team member. It is He, that turns stinking thinking into: Thank You, Jesus.

3. On each widow's birthday, a half a dozen or so members of WONDERS will arrive at the widow's residence to sing "Happy Birthday to You." In hand, they will have a small cake with a lit candle, a helium-filled balloon saying "Happy Birthday," some drinks, ice cream, and a birthday card with a hundred dollars inside. After the singing, we ask if it is all right to put the ice cream in the refrigerator. On one occasion, we discovered a bare refrigerator making us aware that the widow had no food, and we fixed that problem the very next morning. The gift of money is a real shocker to many because they had not even been thought of before. To a widow on a fixed income, this is good news.

4. A WONDERS Christmas dinner is held at a buffet-style restaurant. No one has to cook, and all appetites are satisfied. The widows are all recognized and given small gifts along with a card with a hundred dollars inside.

5. The most important thing we do is provide transportation to church or the doctor's office. We perform small repair jobs needed around the house. We rake and mow the lawn. We wash windows because no eighty-seven-years-old widow should ever be up on a six-foot ladder washing the windows of her house! During winter, we also remove the snow from the walk and driveway.

6. And yes, we teach them the Ten Commandments. The oldest widow to learn the commandments was ninety-three years old. Your WONDERS chapter is a full success when you take a widow to the river and see her

get baptized in the names of the Father, the Son, and the Holy Spirit.

The purposes of WONDERS shall be all that described previously and primarily to:

A. Aid and assist churches and communities in creating and developing ministries called Chapters to provide and serve these purposes.
B. Serve and provide for those widows who are genuinely in need, as determined by Chapters in the churches and communities, and as directed by scriptures, at no cost to the widows.
C. Freely look after orphans and widows in their distress, as determined by Chapters in the churches and communities, and as directed by these scriptures.
D. Reduce the burden placed on churches and communities by donating time, resources, and services for eligible widows and orphans as so determined by Chapters in the churches and communities, and as directed by scriptures.

The concept for Widows Orphans Never Denied Everlasting Reasonable Services, Inc., is to create and support Chapters called WONDERS. The Chapters will help bring awareness to the churches and communities of the identities of widows and orphans who need assistance. The Chapters will then provide those reasonable services if it is within their means and abilities to do so. There is no charge for any services the Chapters may provide. It is strictly the Chapter member's voluntary acts of love serving God's people. It is just that simple.

WONDERS Chapters want to do all that they can for widows and orphans; however, there are limitations. They shall not provide legal or financial counsel, act as power of attorney, give medical advice or care, write checks, apostatize, baptize, or conduct weddings. If any of these are an urgent need, the chapters and churches will recommend or provide a professional from that field if funds are available.

WHAT ABOUT THE MONEY?

When WONDERS started, the church added an account for widows in their record keeping. When people tithe, they are allowed to say where they want their tithes to be applied. WONDERS never charges dues to its members and has never solicited funds from any-one. There are no employees and no one gets paid anything. All monies received are for widows and orphans only.

This book is an example of income. Any income from this book goes directly to the perpetual support of WONDERS, Inc. There is no one making even a penny from this writing.

The King James Bible provides us with two primary examples on how to live as Christians. The first is the life of Jesus, who never sinned. We are to be like Him, to live as He did, without sin.

The second example is how a church should function. Our churches should follow the same examples that are written in the King James Bible.

The church in Jerusalem was the very first to establish a group of seven men to care for the widows, as explained on page one hundred and twenty. But it did not end there. It continued in all of the early churches. Paul started several churches and wrote the following in the first book of Timothy:

> Let not a widow be taken into the number under threescore years old, having been the wife of one man, well reported of for good works; if she have brought up children, if she have lodged strangers, if she have washed the saints' feet, if she have relieved the afflicted, if she have diligently followed every good work.
> (1 Timothy 5:9–10)

Paul also wrote:

> Honor widows that are widows indeed. But if any widow have children or nephews, let them learn first to show piety at home, and to requite their parents: for that is good and acceptable before God. Now she that is a widow indeed, and desolate, trusteth in God, and continueth in supplications and prayers night and day.
> (1 Timothy 5:3–5)

There is no word, from the King James Bible, saying the care, concern and support of the fatherless and widow should ever stop. I seriously challenge all churches to maintain their list of widows over threescore years as mentioned above by Paul. To love them and the fatherless is exactly what Jesus wants us to do. Go do it.

FINAL WORD

Be forewarned that changing our behavior to please our Lord requires personal persistence and perseverance. Our understanding and behavior should be data driven by the words of our Lord in the King James Bible. Our transformation occurs one step at a time, precept upon precept, line upon line, here a little and there a little. Expect that our closest friends and even our family members might not understand the changes in our hearts and minds, now that we have decided to do those things the Lord has asked of us. As you learn the commandments, you may be told such memorization is unnecessary. You may be discouraged from keeping the seventh day Sabbath. When you write the commandments on the post of your house, members of your church may charge you with being legalistic. As you begin to make these changes in your life, the Lord will not leave you but will strengthen your spiritual muscle and your faith in Him.

God is holy, and we are to be holy also. Just like the Sabbath day is to be kept holy and separate from all the other days, we are to separate ourselves from the world. We must be holy in the midst of ungodliness. Our standards should not be dependent upon the shifting moral values of our culture. We cannot believe the messages of "Do your own thing" or "If it feels good, do it" without compromising our relationship with God. Compromise should not be an option for followers of

Christ. God's commandments were kept in a special box known as the Ark of the Covenant. In this context, consider how the phrase "Think outside of the box" would give the option of shying away from His commands. If we love God, we should not be looking for ways around His commandments. Our culture indulges in attitudes and activities that are far from holy. Disrespect for authority is tolerated, sometimes even encouraged. People fulfill their own selfish desires, which can lead to destructive behaviors, many times at the expense of others. Such should not be true for those who love God.

How can we begin to keep the Lord's precepts if we do not know and keep His commandments? They are the backbone of Christianity. Christianity 101. They are the Christian's alphabet. Learning them can be a great beginning for anyone wanting to become a true Christian.

Our Lord only wrote three things in the Bible. First, He authored the Ten Commandments. Second, He wrote: "Mene, Mene, Tekel, Upharsin" upon the plaster of the wall in the king's palace in Babylon. And third, with His finger, He wrote something in the sand defending a harlot. The writing on the wall was lost with the destruction of the king's palace. The writing in the sand vanished long ago in the wind. However, the Ten Commandments were placed in a box called the Ark of the Covenant, located inside the most holy place. God entered the most holy place and sat on the mercy seat, which was on top of the ark. The commandments were so very close to God that the only thing that separated Him from the commandments was His mercy seat. Think about it. We are all dead as sinners and can never live again without forgiveness through God's mercy. We need to turn things around and go back to thinking inside the box. The box and our King James Bible—both homes of the Ten Commandments.

May the person who reads this book learn God's Ten Commandments, word for word, that they may rightfully say,

"Thy word have I hid in mine heart, that I might not sin against Thee."

(Psalm 119:11)

APPENDIX A

How to Love Jesus Quiz Answers

1. Are Christians required to keep the Lord's commandments?
   a. Yes (Leviticus 22:31)

2. The Lord's law, the Ten Commandments, shall be for a sign unto thee if they may be found in thy ____?
   c. Mouth (Exodus 13:9)

3. The Lord bids, commands, us to wear something on the border of our garments to help us remember the commandments. What is it?
   d. A ribbon of blue (Numbers 15:38)

4. Who should teach our children the Ten Commandments?
   d. Their mothers and fathers (Deuteronomy 6:7)

5. When should Christians speak about the commandments?
   e. All of the above (Deuteronomy 6:7)

6. Does the Bible tell us to write the commandments anywhere?
   d. Yes, on the door post of our house (Deuteronomy 6:9)

7. If we observe to do all God's commandments, it shall be our _____?
   d. Righteousness (Deuteronomy 6:25)

8. How close is the Word of God to us?
   d. Both (a) In our mouths and (c) In our hearts (Deuteronomy 30:14)

9. Who was told that the book of the law should not depart from his mouth?
   d. Joshua (Joshua 1:8)

10. Who said the Word of God was in his tongue?
    a. David (2 Samuel 23:1–2)

11. Who never turned back from the commandment of His lips?
    a. Job (Job 23:12)

12. Blessed is the man that does which of these?
    c. Delights in the law of the Lord. (Psalm 1:2)

13. The beginning of wisdom is which of these?
    a. The fear of the Lord. (Psalm 111:10)

14. What shall happen to those who despise the Word of God?
    a. They shall be destroyed. (Proverbs 13:13)

15. What happens when a man turns his ear away from hearing the law?
    d. His prayer shall be abomination. (Proverbs 28:9)

16. What is the whole duty of man?
    e. Both (c) Fear God and (d) Keep His commandments (Ecclesiastes 12:13)

17. Who said: "My words which I have put in thy mouth shall not depart out of thy mouth?"
    d. The Lord (Isaiah 59:21)

18. Jesus said He did not come to destroy the law or the prophets; instead, He came to:
    a. Fulfill (Matthew 5:17)

19. Whosoever shall do and teach the commandments shall be called what in the kingdom of heaven?
    c. Great (Matthew 5:19)

20. Jesus answered the young man, saying, "But if thou will enter into life, _____."
    d. keep the commandments (Matthew 19:17)

21. "He that hath my commandments, and keepeth them, _____."
    e. All of the above (John 14:21)

22. Jesus said you shall abide in His love if you?
    b. Keep His commandments (John 15:10)

23. The scripture says that we do know Him, if we?
    d. Keep His commandments (1 John 2:3)

24. "For this is the love of God, _____"
    d. That we keep His commandments (1 John 5:3)

25. The book of Revelation says, "And the dragon was wroth with the woman, and went to make war with the remnant of her seed, which (fill in this blank), and have the testimony of Je'sus Christ."
    a. Keep the commandments of God (Revelations 12:17)

26. The testimony of Jesus Christ is the spirit of _____?
    b. Prophecy (Revelations 19:10)

27. When the Lord returns, what happens just before we go to be with Him in heaven?
    b. The dead in Christ will rise first (1 Thessalonians 4:16)

28. Near the end of the book of Revelation, it says, "Blessed are they that do His commandments, that they may have right to _____."
    d. The tree of life (Revelations 22:14)

APPENDIX B

Website References

https://biblesabbath.org/
The Bible Sabbath Association

https://www.blueletterbible.org/
The Blue Letter Bible (excellent research site)

http://www.BibleSabbath.org/confessions.html.
"Roman Catholic and Protestant Confessions about Sunday."

http://www.jesus-is-savior.com/False%20Religions/Roman%20Catholicism/2nd_command.htm
"Catholics Remove the 2nd Commandment."

ABOUT THE AUTHOR

After retiring from saving people's lives for almost twenty-eight years in the US Coast Guard, Denny Thomas learned there were many more lost souls needing to be saved, including his own. Around the age of fifty-five, he started reading his Bible every day. He learned the truth about one of the commandments, and it was such a significant spiritual event in his life that he was baptized, a second time, in the river. He read where the King James Bible told him to: "Love the LORD thy God with all thine heart, and with all thy soul, and with all thy might" (Deuteronomy 6:5). He was unable to love the Lord as he had wanted to. He wanted to see Him. He wanted to embrace and hold Him. He wanted to kiss Him and tell Him that he loved Him. But, of course, he could not do that.

After attending various churches for over sixty-five years and never being told or taught how to really love the Lord his God, he found it written right there in his King James Bible. How could this be? How could this most beautiful precept be ignored and not shouted from the rooftops of every church, parish, and synagogue? So, he began to share this "secret" with family, friends, and associates. At the age of seventy-eight, he decided to write this little book to share with others on how to really love the Lord as He describes it Himself. No, it's not what you think, another guy trying to make a fast buck. No, the truth is, every penny from this book goes to aid and support widows and orphans—yes, every penny. His goal is to save one more soul for His kingdom. Learn how to really *love* Him and let the next soul saved be yours.

All profits from this book go directly to Widows and Orphans.